MATCHDOTBOMB

A Midlife Journey through Internet Dating

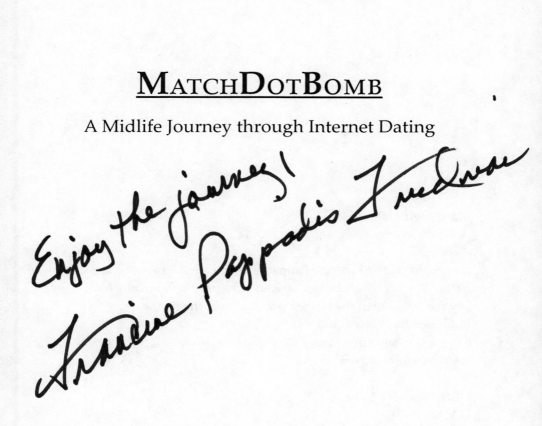

Enjoy the journey!

Francine Pappadis Friedman

FRANCINE PAPPADIS FRIEDMAN

MatchDotBomb
A Midlife Journey through Internet Dating

Published by Wheatmark™
610 East Delano Street, Suite 104, Tucson, Arizona 85705 U.S.A.
www.wheatmark.com

ISBN: 978-1-58736-699-4
LCCN: 2006938865

In Memory

of

Robert

CONTENTS

Introduction

THIS STORY IS TRUE. It is *my* story. And although the fellow travelers with whom I shared my journey are real, I am sure the colors of their characters became more vivid with my memory. Obviously, I have changed their names and identifying details, and have altered even my memories to protect the people of whom my recollections remain pure.

There are 78 million baby boomers in this country, more than 89 million single adults, and over one-third of all the dates in the United States are generated online. I never expected to become a member of this triple statistic simultaneously.

The trip taught me a lot: be open to new adventures, respect other voyagers, leave previous passengers behind, and stow your baggage at the back door. For these valuable lessons and countless other travel tips, I thank the wayfarers I met along the road.

I am grateful to my family and friends, particularly those who encouraged me to share the stories of my dates and then, when they finally stopped laughing, persuaded me to document my experiences. That's how this book evolved.

I am forever indebted to my parents, who always told me to be true to myself. I thought of them often on this journey, along with my daughter and my son, both of whom help me put things into perspective every day. Even as young adults, one's children have a way of doing that.

Finally, this book would not have been written if my late husband had conquered his illness . . . my fondest wish. Ours was a journey unlike any other.

"When you set out on your journey to Ithaca, pray that the road is long, full of adventures, full of knowledge."

—Constantinos Kavafis

1

Solo

IN 1997, MY ONE and only husband died. Every night for the next two years, Larry King's voice lulled me to sleep. In 2000, I started dating an acquaintance but ended the relationship when I realized that the man began his morning golf games on the nineteenth hole. Afterward, my well-meaning friends arranged blind dates for me, which would not have been so bad had I been comatose. I resigned myself to a life of decorating my new condo, immersing myself in my work, and perhaps down the road, starting a new order of nuns with other single women who couldn't bear another fix-up. We could call ourselves the "Sisters of the Blessed Non-Virgin Singles." After all, I had enough female friends who were unattached—by both design and circumstance—to fill a sizable convent. There were scores of us out there . . . solo singles who never married or were divorced or widowed, with and without children. This sounded like a plan.

Thankgivings came and went. I faced Christmas parties alone. I spent the next two New Year's Eves toasting girlfriends and Fred Astaire. I was always the fifth or seventh at the dinner table, wives looking at me askance, as if their paunchy, balding husbands were hot commodities. People had warned me that this would happen.

By mid-January, 2003, those post-holiday blues were pounding at my door. Chicago's temperature was in the single digits as I sat in my drafty office with a wool scarf double-wrapped around my neck. At around two in the afternoon, I received a call from Linda, my dearest friend.

"What are you doing for dinner tonight?" Linda asked excitedly.

"Microwave popcorn at my desk," I replied. "I figure I'll get my carbs, my fiber, and my fat all in one bag."

"No such thing. We're going out for dinner. You, Nancy, and I. We're meeting at Pegasus Restaurant at six-thirty, okay? Gotta run." And with that, she hung up.

This particular girls' night out was neither in my Outlook nor in my weekly planner. My life was predictable: I went to work. I came home. So I was happy to have a reason to leave the office a little early, as I wrote "6:30 dinner/L. & N." on my empty calendar . . . lest I forget.

Linda, Nancy, and I had been friends since high school, an all-girls' Catholic school we affectionately dubbed "Our Lady of Perpetual Agony." They both had helped me survive my freshman year. Now, thirty-six years, five marriages, and seven children later, they were still helping me survive life's trials.

When I arrived at the restaurant, I spotted my two friends across the room huddled in a back booth, poring over what I thought was the menu. Oh those gals, getting a jump on cocktails. As I got closer to the table, I saw that they were reading *The Wall Street Journal*. Please, ladies, no 401(k) talk, I thought. I was depressed enough watching those steadily declining numbers. In fact, I recently had begun to take my accountant's advice: "Francine, throw those quarterly statements in a drawer, unopened. You'll sleep better." His remedy, however, wasn't working, although my sleepless nights may have had more to do with my future than my futures.

As I took off my coat and sat down, these two grown women

began to wave the newspaper in front of my face. Almost in unison, they chanted two frightening words that would mark the beginning of one of the most extraordinary journeys I would ever make: "Internet dating. Internet dating. In-ter-net dat-ing."

I looked first at Linda and then at Nancy and then back at Linda again. Apparently they were serious.

"Oh no, not me. May I remind you of my recent luck with Mr. Bacchanal?" I said.

"Do you mean to tell us that you're going to let old Jim Beam or Jack Daniels—or whatever his name was—poison you against ever getting into another relationship?" Linda asked.

"His name was Barry," I said.

"Whatever. Listen Francine, there's a whole world of eligible men out there in space. You simply need to go cyber shopping. Either that or get on Prozac."

That stung. Did she know that I had just filled the prescription that I had been carrying around in my wallet for the last three months? Not that I had taken any of the pills yet. I could tough it out. I was convinced that these blues were a form of seasonal affective disorder. I just needed to pick up a few fluorescent lamps and I'd be fine.

"Look, ladies, I may not be wildly happy, but I'm content. And you can make fun of my cautious nature all you want, but at least I'm *alive*. I've read those accounts of women's bodies found in the forest preserves with their pantyhose wrapped around their necks and the personal ads still tucked in their purses. No thanks. Uh, uh. Absolutely not," I protested.

An hour and a half and two bottles of wine later, my happily (well, one not so happily) married friends would not relent. They were convinced that this was the answer to my loneliness. Unlike speed dating (a term that I—a product of the sixties—assumed had something to do with amphetamines when I first heard of it), Internet dating, they assured me, was relaxing. Unlike lunch dates (for a woman who barely has time for a carton of yogurt at her desk), this, they promised, could be done at one's leisure. Then a strange phenomenon occurred. With a demonic look in her eyes and a voice like Linda Blair's in *The Exorcist*, Nancy said, "If you don't sign yourself up, we'll sign up for you, submit your picture, and write your profile . . . and then you'll be sorry." I sat there, waiting for her head to start spinning around. I was *already* sorry. My best friends were blackmailing me—for my own good, of course.

Then it began. They regaled me with stories of friends of acquaintances or acquaintances of friends who had found their true loves on the Internet.

"My cousin's coworker has been dating this great guy she met a year ago online. Last month, he even got his tattoo removed just for her, and I understand that the procedure is excruciating. Now *that's* real love," said Linda.

"And I know a woman whose divorce papers were barely filed by her husband before she had more Internet dates than she knew what to do with. In fact, her attorney told her to slow down and try to act a little more like the aggrieved party . . . for the sake of her settlement," added Nancy.

"Girls, I'm looking for quality, not quantity," I said.

The two of them rolled their eyes, four brows arching in cadence. Their banter continued, and my head started to throb.

"Okay. At the very most, I'll read the article," I promised. "But that's all." I put the paper in my briefcase, and took out my wallet to settle the bill. I was exhausted and desperately wanted to go home.

"No. This one's on me," said Linda with a glint in her eye as she grabbed the check.

We said our good-byes in the parking lot and I got into my car and popped my newest Tony Bennett CD in the player to drown out the evening. "Every Day I Have the Blues" . . . God, he could sing. As I pulled into my garage, he had just begun to croon, "Alright, Okay, You Win." Tony, are you speaking to me or to my friends? I was feeling anxious.

I shuffled into the elevator and leaned against the back wall. I had drunk too much wine. I stared up at the digital numbers that displayed the floors. The elevator door finally opened on mine, and I tottered down the hall to my apartment, unlocked the door, and then double-locked it behind me. The quiet was so piercing that, for a moment, I thought I could actually hear the air in the living room as I walked in and turned on the lights. I peeled off my clothes and headed for a long, steamy bubble bath. As I was soaking, the phone rang and the answering machine clicked on.

"I know you're there," Linda's voice said. "You're probably in the tub. I just hung up with Nancy five minutes ago. Now listen. We know you better than you know yourself, and we promise that this is going to be the right thing for you. We'll talk tomorrow."

How did she know I was in the tub? After fifteen minutes of watching the bubbles disappear around me like some of my loved ones had, I stood up, wrapped myself in a towel, and went through my nightly ritual of brushing, flossing, exfoliating, and slathering with gobs of body lotion. I crawled—slipped, actually—into bed and turned off the light, anticipating a big day at work on Friday, including two meetings in the morning and a proposal to finish writing. I had to get some sleep. After tossing for an hour, trying to get comfortable in a bed that had grown so much larger in the last half-dozen years, I turned on the light, propped up two pillows, and reached for my briefcase. I always kept it on the floor right next to my side of the bed, which was *either* side now. I pulled out the *Journal* article and began reading.

2

The Launch

PREPARING FOR THE WORLD of Internet dating was, for me, similar to getting ready for a job interview. I assessed my qualifications and experiences and then determined how to go about presenting myself in the best light, or more accurately, the brightest glow of the computer screen.

I used a legal pad, listing my strengths and weaknesses, my likes and dislikes, and my goals and objectives. I had made lists my entire life—for all of my major decisions, save one. I chose who I would vote for in presidential elections using this method. Before I bought a car, my legal pad was divided into two columns, with Toyota on the left and Honda on the right. I ended my last relationship when the "con" list heavily outnumbered the "pro." The only time list making never entered my mind was when I married three decades ago. I jumped in with my whole heart and soul and never looked back.

For my online debut, I needed three things: a cyber name, a headline, and a profile. I started with a good moniker, as I was warned never to use my real name when creating my Internet persona. A cyber name could be a nickname, a favorite town, an ice cream flavor, an acronym, a literary character . . . anything at all. "Olivia Viola" became my Internet identity.

Next, I attempted to create a clever, captivating headline. I discovered scores of catchy titles floating out there in cyberspace. "Alto Seeks Baritone," "Goldilocks Looking for Her Teddy Bear," "Dancer Needs Partner," and "Avid Jogger Tired of Running Solo" were a few of my favorites. I chose "Girl Next Door," although I worried that the word "girl" was a bit misleading.

Then I had to create my profile, which is analogous to a resume. I began with just the facts . . . where I lived (city and state, never the exact address), my age, my marital status, if I had and/or wanted children, the color of my hair and eyes, my height and weight, languages spoken, religion, education, profession, salary range, and so on. From there, I composed my personal narrative. This was my opportunity to whet the appetites of the men of cyber world with a morsel of intriguing information, giving them a taste of my personality and hopefully leaving them hungry for more. After describing myself, I stated what qualities I was seeking in my ideal match, hoping to attract candidates for candid dates . . . honest, upfront men whose bullshit-ometers wouldn't start running from the moment they said hello. And finally, I included a recent photo of myself. "You will receive eight times as many responses if you post your photo," say the Internet dating gods.

It took me approximately four hours to write my profile. It was an exercise in taking stock of myself and it was therapeutic, if nothing else. But it was *not* nothing else. It made me really think about who I was, what I liked and didn't like, and where I wanted to go and with whom. Seeing my photo and profile online made me feel real and tangible in a world that too often seems vague and surreal.

Writing a personal narrative was not easy. Allow me to share some advice in two words: Be truthful. If you're honest during this arduous exercise, you'll never regret it, assuming that honesty is what you're after. In fact, most often you'll get what you give, including double-entendres or suggestive come-ons, which are fine, if that's what you want. If you're forty-five years old but look thirty-seven, list your age as forty-five. (I eliminated candidates from the onset whom I suspected had lied about their age. You know, the guy in his "early forties" who slips about his teenage grandchildren). If you're overweight, don't list your body type as "slim/slender," unless you're planning to put Internet dating on hold for six months while you stick to some torturous diet. If you're separated but not yet divorced, say so. If you hate opera, don't list it among your favorite types of music to appear erudite. Fabrication and presenting yourself in the best light are two different things. There are basic rules to follow when composing your profile . . . the same ones that apply to life: "To Thine Own Self Be True" and "Do unto Others as You Would Have Them Do unto You."

These rules also should assist you in your search, "should" being the operative word here. There'll be some hidden glitches along the way, but knowing what you're looking for will help you narrow the field as you review hundreds of candidates' profiles. It all comes down to choices. Although beauty is only skin deep, let's remember how much skin a Shar-Pei has. If someone describes himself as "athletic" but his photo reveals him to be Pavarotti's twin brother, at least you can make an educated choice. In fact, some women prefer beefy men. If a guy's headline reads, "Wears My Hard on My Sleeve," you can choose whether or not to make contact—and with what part of the body. I'm not passing judgment. It's all about choices.

Likewise, questions about one's ideal place to live, housekeeping habits, fashion style, sense of humor, religion, political views, hobbies, musical preferences, pets, and my personal favorite: "turn-ons and turn-offs." You'd be amazed—and appalled—at some of the responses to this last query. Many times, just as I was about to click EMAIL THIS PERSON when viewing a candidate's adorable photo or catchy cyber name, I was saved after carefully reviewing his profile. Data was the key here.

When I read "I'll tell you later" as the answer to "marital status," I automatically deleted. Come on, guys, what could you possibly be thinking? When I saw "atheist" in response to "religion," I got a little concerned. I mean, if I didn't have some kind of faith, would I even be submitting myself to the world of Internet dating? Of course, that's just my opinion. When I read "other" listed for hair color, I knew exactly what to expect. I personally find bald men sexy. My father, who was fifty years old when I was born, was baldheaded from the first day we met—the one day our looks had the most in common—and I considered him the most gallant gentleman I would ever know. Yet, as much as my father disliked being maneless and tried some hilarious remedies to stimulate hair follicles (my favorite was washing his head over the kitchen sink with fresh spinach leaves), he didn't succumb to hair weaves, plugs, or comb-overs, the last of which can be rather risky in the Windy City. On the other hand, some women may prefer that wrap-around hairdo to a gleaming, shiny head. Again, it's all about choices.

When a prospect listed his primary hobby as "skeet shooting," I had a choice. I pressed DELETE. When the response to "have children?" was "tell you later!" as far as I was concerned, he needn't bother. When "ferrets" was the answer to "have pets?" my rejoinder was "thanks, but no thanks." When the reply to "ideal residence" was "cabin in the country," I was inclined to move on, as I relish gazing at the city's skyline from my condo in the clouds.

When the person admitted to being a slob, I applauded his candor. Ditto when he listed his annual salary as $18,000. It was all about information gathering, sorting, setting priorities, and making choices that were right for *me*. I'll admit that this became challenging when I was not receiving honest answers. But with practice and several email chats, I quickly learned to discern fact from fiction. And although it made me feel vulnerable, I wrapped my own personal package in transparent paper and tied it with a ribbon of reality, embracing the Internet daters' mantra: "Give truth and ye shall receive it."

The following is my abbreviated Internet profile—the one that was viewed by 9,978 people—which elicited 337 responses. (The Internet service keeps track for you.) No, I didn't go on 337 dates, or I never would have had the time to write this book. But I did meet a patchwork of candidates with a myriad of interests—some toting their baggage in small nylon satchels that would fit easily under the seats in front of them, others dragging steamer trunks. And I remained ever hopeful that one of them would be a perfect match. Optimistic? Naive? Stupid? Whatever the adjective, I was out there in cyberspace and there was no turning back.

So come along on this voyage, as I describe some real dating experiences—changing names and specific details to protect my fellow hopefuls, of course. As you meet some of my dates, you will undoubtedly ask why I kept returning to the keyboard. I asked myself that same question at the end of many an afternoon or evening engagement. (I don't do mornings). Yet, as I traveled down this road, the answer became obvious: "What's the alternative?" Life, after all, is a journey, with peaks and valleys. Giving up never even crossed my mind. And besides, the hoot factor alone was worth the trip.

My Profile

"Olivia Viola"/ Girl Next Door		Seeks: Regular Guy	
ABOUT ME:		**ABOUT YOU:**	
AGE:	54	AGE:	48 to 60
CITY/STATE:	Chicago, IL	LOCATION:	Within 20 miles radius
STATUS:	Widowed	STATUS:	Never married, divorced, widowed
BODY TYPE:	Slim/slender	BODY TYPE:	Slim, average, husky
HAIR/EYES:	Brown/Green	HAIR/EYES:	Any/Any color
SALARY:	Tell you later	SALARY:	Open
OCCUPATION:	Degreed Professional	OCCUPATION:	Professional/Open
CHILDREN:	Grown, not living at home	CHILDREN:	Any, grown

My Profile

My friends would say that I am loyal, considerate, bright, and energetic with a great sense of humor and style. I enjoy all types of music, from jazz and classical to rock and everything in between . . . except country. (Sorry, Garth). I like movies, concerts, theatre, opera, reading everything from biographies to the latest novels (no sci-fi, please), and I love to write. I'm comfortable in all types of social settings, from black-tie galas to backyard barbecues. I've traveled quite a bit, and hope to do more. Are there any quality gentlemen out there interested in a friendship that could develop into something more? If so, give me a cyber whistle—and don't forget to bring those all-important ingredients: kindness, honesty, accountability, generosity of spirit, and a sense of humor. After all, it's no fun if we can't laugh!

3

Shelly

I WAS WELL AWARE THAT I was going to have to shed a lifetime of memories of my late husband, Bob, or—at the very least—tuck them far away where they couldn't creep into every date. Otherwise, it simply wouldn't be fair to all of these hopeful matches or to me.

This was going to be a challenge. I had met Bob when I was sixteen. When I first laid eyes on him, he was doing pushups behind the stage of my all-girls high school auditorium. I was the president of our drama club and we relied on thespian-bent guys from the 'hood to take on the male parts in our school productions.

Bob was into physical fitness, and he loved the theatre. And, like any red-blooded guy, he also loved girls. And speaking of love, the sight of him dropping to the floor to exercise in between acts was so outrageous, so out there, that I was immediately smitten.

Bob was a few years older than I, much to my parents' dismay. I was the baby in the family and my father, especially, wanted to keep it that way for a few more years. But the attraction was powerful on all levels and even when our attending colleges in different states separated us, we managed to find twenty-nine dollar round-trip flights, take trains, or borrow roommates' cars—whatever it took to be together, even if only for a weekend. During my sophomore year, we eloped. I moved back to Chicago where I continued going to school in the city, and we started a family. It took my parents awhile to get over the fact that their youngest child had launched into marriage before getting her degree, but when the grandchildren began to arrive, they relented. Besides, it didn't take long for everyone to figure out that I simply had married a younger version of my father—just one without the big, fat, Greek accent.

Our love was profound. And there was humor in everything. Bob was one of the few people who could find something funny in any situation. Not to the point of total irreverence, mind you. He did have a serious side. But sitting down and watching the nightly news with him was like going to a comedy club. His one-liners softened the rough world and tough times. I thought that we'd grow old rocking and rollicking together. I was wrong.

I was wrong about something else, too. I never thought that three decades later, I would be moving on . . . to my very first cyber date, Shelly, a native New Yorker who had settled in Chicago.

You can take the boy out of the Bronx, but you can't take the Bronx out of the boy. I like New York. I like New Yorkers, despite the fact that, years ago on my first trip to New York City, I stopped a young man on the street and asked him if he could tell me the correct time, only to have him walk away as he yelled back at me, "My fault ya ain't got a watch, girlie?" I'll never forget that guy.

When Shelly emailed me, I was intrigued. Shelly was an East Coast transplant who had been living in Chicago for the last twenty years. His emails were short. To the point. No wasted verbiage here. Did I want to have dinner? Straight to the chase. Of course I did.

"How about nine o'clock next Thursday night?" Shelly wrote. I was encouraged. Like me, he obviously was a night owl. No early-bird specials for Shelly. This was a cosmopolitan guy who was probably still operating on Eastern Standard Time.

"Great," I emailed back.

We exchanged our work numbers and talked several times during the week. In our first few conversations, I often found myself interrupting Shelly with "Pardon me?" or "Could you repeat that?" Shelly spoke faster than a drive-by bullet. It became a challenge to keep up the verbal pace. And I loved a good challenge.

We agreed to meet at one of Shelly's favorite restaurants, an Italian joint on Taylor Street where everyone knew him. In fact, he had instructed me that if I was the first to arrive, I should tell Vincent, the maitre d,' that I was there to meet Shelly. I did, and Vincent ushered me to a table by the window that had a card that said Reserved on it. As I sat down, Vincent stealthily slipped the card into his breast pocket, took my drink order, and came back with my glass of wine and a plate of piping hot, stuffed mushrooms.

"Compliments of our chef, Antonio," said Vincent. "Antonio is the best chef in the U.S. of A. His homemade gnocchi is better than my mama's. His lasagna is . . ." and with this, Vincent put his fingers to his lips and sprayed the air with a kiss. "Antonio's a genius in the kitchen."

"Is Antonio single?" I asked.

Vincent looked at me and walked away.

Within five minutes, Shelly arrived. I recognized him as soon as he entered the restaurant because his sophisticated stance looked as if he had walked right off of a page of a Bloomingdale's catalogue. He was wearing a gorgeous silk suit, a cream-colored shirt, and a tie that resembled a tiny slice of a stained glass window, a tie that he probably purchased at the Museum of Modern Art. Vincent pointed in my direction.

"Francine?" Shelly inquired.

"Shelly," I replied.

Before Shelly was seated, the waiter had placed a giant martini in front of him. Shelly held it up to my almost-full glass of wine and said, "To your health . . . and to us."

Us. It had such a nice ring to it. Not since my marriage had anyone referred to me as "us," the partner in my last relationship having spoken exclusively in the first person singular. I was feeling lightheaded, and I'd only had two sips of wine. Careful.

The food kept coming as if this were our very own last supper which, as I look back now, was quite prophetic. Time to get to know one another, I thought. I began.

"Have you been alone long, Shelly?"

"You mean lately?" he asked.

"Well, yes, in this millennium," I answered, trying to sound clever to mask my anxiety.

"I've been divorced now for four years from my third wife, Pandy," Shelly replied.

"Pandy?" I repeated, raising an eyebrow.

"Yeah. Short for Pandora. Too bad I hadn't studied mythology in high school a little more . . . maybe I could've avoided that box of horrors. Pandy Smith. Ya know her? She never took my last name, which was just as well 'cause the ink was barely dry on the marriage certificate before it was all over."

Better for her had she taken his first name, I thought. "I'm sorry," I said.

"By the second year of our marriage, she was having an affair with someone," Shelly went on. "I knew it, 'cause every time I walked into the room when she was on the phone, she pretended she was ordering groceries and hung up real fast. Funny thing, though. The groceries never came. How dumb did she think I was?"

Okay, let's move on, I said to myself.

"That was your third wife?" I asked.

"Yeah. I was married for twenty-three years, if you add 'em all up. Twelve years the first time around. I knew Cindy and I were headed south right after my second daughter was born, but I was working like a dawg, the kids were little, and I was trying to be a good dad, so I hung in there."

A good dad. I like that, I thought to myself, trying to cling to something positive.

"So how many children do you have, Shelly?"

"Three all together. All girls. Two from my first marriage and one from my second. But I'd rather not go into those seven years of hell, if ya don't mind. The older daughters live in New Jersey, and the youngest is in Chicago."

"Oh, how nice for you to have one of them living right here in town. Do you get together with her often?" I asked.

"Haven't seen her in two and a half years. Bawl's in her court," he replied.

Now, I get into spats with my kids, too, I thought. Not two-year squabbles, mind you, but it's none of my business. Business. Now there's a topic.

"What kind of work do you do, Shelly?"

"Financial advisor. Been in the field for thirty years. But I refuse to have any schmucks for clients. Life's too short, ya know what I mean?"

I suddenly did. "So, how's business?" I asked.

"Business is great. Actually couldn't be better, except that my secretary up and quit today. Just after I trained her for the past eight months! I shoulda known somethin' was goin' on. Every time she went out for a coffee break or to the bathroom, she took her cell phone with her. I'm puttin' an ad in this weekend's paper for a new secretary. This time I'll call it 'administrative assistant.' Twenty-two secretaries in thirty years. This sucks!"

Yes, I agreed to myself, translating "sucks" into "pattern." Nonetheless, I tried to be empathic.

"I could help you write the job ad, Shelly. I'm a writer, you know."

"Thanks, but I'm just pulling up the one I used eight months ago."

Right. I forgot. He undoubtedly had the editor of the *Tribune*'s job section on retainer.

"You look very nice, Shelly," I said, figuring maybe this guy needed a little TLC.

"Thanks. I just got a haircut. My regular barber hasn't been able to fit me into his 'busy schedule' for the past few months. So I've been going to his partner. But get this: last Monday when his partner cut my hair, my regular barber was sittin' in the next chair readin' *Sports Illustrated*. Just sittin' there. So, how busy can his schedule really be, huh? I'm not even gonna request my regular barber anymore. I'm gonna treat him with the same disdain that he treats me with."

I had never heard the words "disdain" and "barber" in the same sentence before, but I suppose there's a first time for everything.

Continuing on this *King and I* "Getting to Know You" journey, I said, "So tell me, Shelly, do you have brothers and sisters?"

"I have a sister who's living in Atlanta, last I heard. I haven't seen her in eighteen years. We never did get along very well."

"Oh, I'm sorry," I said.

"Don't be. I'm not. Unfortunately, ya can't pick your relatives."

The rest of the dinner was spent engaging in small talk. Small, angry talk. Shelly's business partner was out to get him, his garage attendant carelessly scratched his car's bumper, his cleaning lady ruined his carpet, he was never going to call an old friend again, and on and on and on.

Now, I can sympathize with failure, frustration, and heartbreak. I can relate to anxiety and insecurity. And I can even accept small doses of its common side effect, pretense. But I have a difficult time with gratuitous anger. Maybe because I've seen *real* rage—the deadly kind—and I never again want to be near anything that even remotely resembles it. I'm looking for someone who loves life as much as I . . . someone who sees the humorous side of almost every situation . . . someone who, albeit foolishly at times, gives everyone the benefit of at least one doubt.

As he walked me to my car, Shelly said that he'd keep in touch. And as I turned to say good night to him for the first and last time, I had the strangest feeling we had met before.

Driving home, I thought about some of the malcontents I'd encountered in my life. I suddenly recalled my first visit to New York. That was it. There was a certain resemblance between that young man on the street in New York City years ago—the one who wouldn't give me the time of day—and Shelly. Just a coincidence, I'm sure.

I didn't check my messages when I arrived home from my date with Shelly. I was too exhausted. The veteran online daters say that the first one takes a lot out of you. All I remember doing is going home, brushing my teeth, and falling into bed.

At seven the next morning, I leaned over to hit the snooze button, but the alarm wouldn't stop beeping. Wait, it was my phone ringing. Who was calling me at this hour? Everyone who knows me knows that I'm incoherent until nine.

"Hello," I mumbled.

"Thank God you're alright." It was Linda on the other end. "Didn't you get any of my messages?" she continued.

"What messages?"

"I left you three messages on your machine last night. I stopped calling after eleven. You said that you had a date with some fellow Internetter, and all I could imagine is that you had been kidnapped and were being driven down to Mexico in some guy's trunk," she went on.

"Oh, sure. *Now* you're concerned. Where were you and Nancy when you strong-armed me into signing up for this journey? Listen, I've gotta get going. I have a big meeting at work at ten. The guy was not for me. I'll fill you in later," I replied.

"As long as you're okay. I was going to call the police—or at least your doorman—if you didn't answer this morning," she went on.

"Linda, did it ever occur to you that the date might have been so fantastic that I ended up spending the night at his place?" I asked.

"Oh, please. You're not the type," she said matter-of-factly.

She was right.

Linda, on the other hand, *was* the type in her single days. She wasn't promiscuous. She just grabbed what she wanted, while I always had that old Catholic school guilt running through my non-Catholic veins. With my limited dating experience, I couldn't even *imagine* sleeping with more men in my lifetime than I could

count on one hand. Nor could I understand timeshare relationships. I even had a tough time grasping serial monogamy. After
all, when I got married thirty-some years ago, it was for better or
for worse, for richer or for poorer, in sickness and in health, till
death do us part.

I just never counted on that death part.

4

Stages

WHEN IT CAME TO dating, I was totally out of practice. I'm not saying that after several years of grieving Bob's death, I proceeded directly from *Larry King Live* to my computer contestants.

In between, there *were* some dates with a few non-online men whom I'd prefer to forget. Psychologists refer to this as selective memory. Laymen call it "What was I thinking?" Nonetheless, I suppose one could say that I was going through a few stages before I succumbed to the pressure of journeying through cyberspace.

I'll begin chronologically with my former colleague, Joe, a man with whom I had worked for a half-dozen years. Joe was kind, smart, humorous, and married. And he was old enough to be my father or, at the very least, my uncle. As I recall those days now, however, "Uncle" Joe treated me very nicely but never very niecely.

We had a few things in common, Joe and I. When I began working with him, I had been married for over twenty years. Joe had been married forever. I had two children. Joe had four. I had a mortgage. So did Joe. I had a devoted husband whom I loved. Joe worshipped his adoring wife. The only thing that Joe had that

I didn't, besides the obvious, were grandchildren—five of them—and about nineteen years on me. And another major difference that wouldn't surface until years later: I never, ever had the hots for Father Joseph.

In all of the years that I worked with Joe, our relationship was strictly professional. We respected one another. We liked each other's spouses, the four of us exchanging mindless pleasantries at those interminable, obligatory work-related activities that threw us together. Joe was a pleasant, supportive, appropriately friendly coworker. He never failed to share photographs of his latest vacation with his wife, Christine, or pictures of their grandchildren on the brood's most recent visit to "Nana and Poppy's" house. It was a platonic relationship and, for those six years on the job, I felt valued, admired, respected, and, most of all, safe.

During year five, Christine was diagnosed with a rare neurological disease and Joe was devastated. He turned into a totally different man: broken, distracted, sullen, angry—and very needy. My other colleagues and I understood. Joe and Christine had been walking down the same path in life for over forty years and, suddenly, a detour sign appeared out of nowhere. Joe was helpless. He became pale, thin, and humorless. His breakfast was black coffee at his desk. Lunch was a bowl of soup. He'd leave work early to pick up some fast food for himself, which he'd eat at Christine's bedside. It was a quick demise for Christine, who lived for only four months after her diagnosis. And, at about the same time that Joe lost Christine, he lost me to another company. It was an unplanned, if ill-timed, departure but it was simply an offer that, as they say, I couldn't refuse. And besides, Joe was a professional acquaintance—nothing more.

I kept in touch with a few of my former colleagues, including Joe. He and I would chat on the phone once or twice a year around the holidays, engaging in small talk about our kids, his grandkids, and his loneliness. Then, as often happens, I completely lost track of most of my past coworkers, including Joe. I was consumed with my new job, trying to balance it with my personal life and, shortly thereafter, to deal with Bob's illness.

It wasn't until years later—four to be exact—that I heard from Joe. He had learned of Bob's death from a mutual friend, having missed the obituary that had appeared in the newspaper about ten days earlier, and he was calling to pay his respects. Actually, it turned out that Joe was multitasking: it was a condolence-and-let's-go-out-for-dinner call. I wasn't offended. In those first few weeks, my family and friends had been filling my lonely hours on a daily basis. Dinner with an old colleague seemed harmless to me. I didn't realize at the time that Joe considered it a date.

"How about Printer's Gallery? They're having a cocktail reception and art auction," he suggested. It sounded like a pleasant distraction. Curiously, I offered to meet him there, wanting to have my own car as an escape device. Reassuring? Maybe. Clairvoyant? Perhaps.

We met at the gallery. Joe looked quite dapper. There was an hour's preview before the art auction and, while we grazed on hors d'oeuvres, Joe admired several modern paintings, especially one of an ample woman sitting by a window that he said would look particularly striking on his dining room wall.

"This artist was one of Christine's favorites," he went on to explain to me, who was clueless about contemporary art. I personally thought it atrocious but dismissed my own opinion as unsophisticated and elementary.

When the auction began, so did Joe's tell. Almost everyone has one—that sign that's a dead giveaway or, at the very least, a hint of some anxiety or stress. For some, it's a foot tapping on the floor; for others, it's twirling a few strands of hair; for Joe, it was rapid, successive blinks of his right eye. Never the left. Always the right. I had observed his tell for years in the workplace. Once, when a confrontational board member implied that Joe's leadership skills were slipping, Joe's eyelid started fluttering like a butterfly's wings and, for a moment, I thought that he was having a petit mal seizure. Another time, when he and I were meeting with a vendor who had unfairly inflated her invoice, I initially thought that Joe was winking at me repeatedly until I realized that he had caught on to the con and simply could not control his fury or his pulsating lid.

Back at the art gallery, Joe was going to be the successful bidder of the wide-woman-by-the-window painting if it killed him—or depleted his bank account, whichever happened first. The curator's assistant lifted up the portrait, and the bidding began at fourteen hundred dollars. A young man raised his arm.

"Do I hear sixteen hundred?" the auctioneer asked.

With right eye twitching, Joe held up his hand.

"Do I hear eighteen hundred?" the auctioneer goaded. The young man nodded.

Joe raised two fingers and one trembling brow. His competitor frowned.

"I have two thousand from the gentleman in the back," the auctioneer said, acknowledging Joe.

An elderly lady in the front row gasped and turned around to see what idiot would pay two grand for a portrait of a chubby woman bordered by a cheesy metal frame, the kind that could be picked up at Wal-Mart for about fifteen bucks.

"A magnificent watercolor. Do I hear twenty-two? Twenty-two? Two thousand going once. Two thousand going twice. Sold to the gentleman in the back," said the auctioneer with a gleam in his eye, which was steady and unwavering, as he slammed down his gavel.

Joe got up and I followed him to the vestibule, where people were settling their bills and collecting their art. He pulled out his checkbook and wrote "two thousand and no one hundreds."

"Congratulations, Joe, on your great steal," I lied.

"Thanks, Christine. It'll look great in the dining room, don't you think?" he asked.

How the hell would I know? I had never been inside of Joe and Christine's house in all the years I'd known them.

"*Francine*," I corrected him.

"That's what I said," Joe replied. "Don't you think it'll be perfect in our dining room?"

Uh-oh.

"I don't know, Joe. I've never seen your dining room. But I'm sure that it will look lovely," I answered.

"You really do, don't you? Listen, why don't we get our coats and you follow me home in your car? You could help me position the painting just right."

I didn't want to follow him anywhere, and I especially didn't want to hear the word *position* in his invitation.

"Oh, I don't think so, Joe. I have to get home. It's getting late. But thanks for a nice evening," I said, as we started to walk outside toward our respective cars.

"Maybe this weekend, then. I could wait until Saturday or Sunday to hang it. Do you have plans this weekend, Christine?" he asked, as his right eye began to quiver.

"*Francine*," I said again. "Yes, I do. I'm awfully busy."

"Oh. I just thought, we're both alone and everything, that maybe you'd like to come over. The grandkids won't be visiting for another month, and the place is so big. I know it's a far drive, but you could stay over . . . I mean in the spare bedroom, of course," Joe went on, his right lashes flickering in the evening breeze.

"Thanks, Joe," I said, "but I have so much to do this weekend." What with Bob's body still warm, I thought.

"Okay, maybe in a few weeks. I'll give you a call," Joe replied.

He leaned down to kiss me on the lips, but I lowered my head so that his mouth brushed my forehead, turning his caress into a sweet peck a father would give his daughter. I gave him a hug and told him to be well, sensing that I probably would never see him again. I was right.

As I drove away, I realized that while Joe's soul was still smarting from the loss of Christine, his body undoubtedly was ready to launch into another relationship. While his eye was twitching, his libido was itching. He had been widowed for more than a few years, whereas I had been widowed for a few weeks. Joe had loads of time on his hands and his healthy appetite for life had returned. I, on the other hand, had a stack of things on my plate, with a heaping pile of grief at the top of the dish. Yet even if we had been on the same schedule, it wouldn't have worked between Joe and me. That evening—the one he considered a date, while I considered it dinner with an old friend—was the first and last for the two of us.

Nine months after Bob's death, my world was rocked once again. My brother, Tommy, who thought he had a bad case of the flu, was diagnosed with advanced stages of pancreatic cancer. In a state of shock, I alternated from going through the motions of work by day to visiting Tommy by night, with surfing the Internet in between for the latest, innovative medical treatment that could save him. There was none. All I could do was be there for him . . . and wait for the inevitable.

A week later, I had an appointment to see my accountant, Marv. Tax filing extension time was looming once again, and for the second consecutive year, I arrived at his office with a shopping bag of forms and receipts that I had been collecting. It was out of character for me, who usually had everything neatly arranged in my alphabetized accordion folder. I also had been putting off tying up all of the loose ends that one needs to do after a spouse's death.

"What about insurance policies?" Marv asked. "Don't forget to fill out the forms for your widow's pension. Was there a mortgage pay-off policy? What about your will?"

I knew that all of these things were important, but as I sat across the desk from Marv, I simply broke down. I couldn't deal with any of this. I couldn't move—I was frozen. I didn't care about taxes, insurance, pensions, or any other policies. And I knew something else: Bob and I didn't have a will.

"*What*?" Marv said, as he leaned forward. "What longtime married couple with grown children doesn't have a will?"

"A lot of people don't," I countered, feeling like a total fool. "Please don't lecture me," I retorted.

"Francine, I'm sorry. I know you're under a lot of stress. But it's been almost a year now, and you're the only parent your children have left. You need to take care of these things. Listen, I can give you the name of a good lawyer who specializes in wills and estates—unless you have someone else you'd rather go to."

"No, I don't have anyone else," I said, fighting back tears.

"Okay, then take this name, Tim Lyon, and give him a call," Marv said, as he handed me a piece of paper he had scribbled on. "He's a good guy. Irish Catholic. About our age. A family man. Call him as soon as you can, alright?"

Suddenly, I was feeling very tiny in Marv's office, amidst stacks of papers piled on his credenza and the floor; file cabinets with numbered reference books sitting on top, mostly out of sequence; a Mr. Coffee that looked like it hadn't been cleaned in a year; and a Mickey Mouse mug, the handle of which was the celebrated rodent's right ear.

"Marv, I can't do this," I said.

"Do what?"

"Any of this. I need someone to take care of everything."

"Then, Tim's your man. Look, I haven't spoken to him in a while, but I'll call him, give him a heads up, and ask him to phone you this week. Would that help if *I* got the ball rolling?" Marv asked.

"I guess so," I replied, feeling like I was shrinking by the minute.

About a week later, my phone rang at work. "Timothy Lyon, here," said a soft voice at the other end.

"Timothy who?" I asked, confused and distracted, as my assistant had just handed me a report that I needed to review for my nine o'clock meeting the following morning.

"Tim Lyon. I'm a business acquaintance of your accountant, Marv Green. Marv said that you were in need of an attorney to help you handle some matters. If you've already taken care of things, I understand."

"No, I haven't done anything. I just can't do any of it. Can you help me?" I blurted.

"I think so, Francine. Let's start at the beginning."

And with that, Tim Lyon and I *did* start—a very long telephone relationship that gave phone sex a new, innocent meaning.

Tim called me every afternoon at work. If I was about to leave my office to visit Tommy, he said he'd catch me at home later in the evening, which he always did. We'd talk till nine or ten at night—about our lives, our families, our kids, our jobs, and my brother. I asked him if the meter was running. He always said, "Not for you, Franny." I asked him what he was doing working so late every night. He said he was happier at work than at home. I asked him where home was. He said that it was an apartment about a mile from his office. I asked him if he was divorced. He said he was separated. "Legally?" I queried. "I'm Catholic," he replied.

And so it began. Was Tim Lyon lyin'? I didn't know and cared even less. My husband had died a year earlier and my brother would be gone in a matter of months. I needed someone to take care of things and of me and, as Marv had said, Tim was my man.

Tim and I did not actually meet until about six weeks after our first telephone conversation, about thirty phone calls and ninety billable hours later. I spoke with Tim almost every afternoon and weeknight, but never on weekends. One evening, he suggested that we finally meet on the following Friday night for a drink. We described ourselves to one another. Tim said that he was about six feet four, with blue eyes and dark brown, curly hair. "Very curly," he said. "In fact, when my friends aren't poking fun at my height by calling me 'Tiny,' they dub me 'Curly.'" I was certain that I'd recognize this man among a hundred others in the room.

We met for the first time at a little Chinese restaurant in the Loop. I walked right over to him at the bar, amidst about a dozen other guys. He was tall, even sitting down. And I spotted that dark curly hair and the light blue eyes the minute I saw them.

We took a small booth in the back of the restaurant, and Tim slid in next to me. The currents were flying, as we spent another three hours talking about everything. I felt as though I had known Tim Lyon my entire life. Neither one of us wanted to leave, but he said that he had to get back to the office the next morning, as he was working on a big case. That was the beginning of our Friday night dates.

Was it a coincidence that the first time Tim and I spent the night together was on the eve of my brother's death? I had visited Tommy every day after he had entered the hospital for the final time. On this particular one—his last, although it was unbeknownst to all of us—I didn't go to work so that I could spend the entire day with him. When every other family member left his room to get something to eat, I stayed behind, the mere thought of food nauseating to me. Tommy was unresponsive, having slipped into a coma the night before; but, still, I hoped he could hear me. I told him that I loved him, and I put my mouth right up against his ear and sang softly to him, "The Bells of St, Mary's, I hear them a-calling. . . ." It was a song that my father used to sing to us when we were young while Tommy accompanied him on the piano, and I sensed that they'd soon be together.

Tim picked me up from the hospital at around eleven that night and drove me home. Before going up to my apartment, we took a walk along the beach. It was a sizzling summer evening, the humidity sticky and thick as honey. We climbed up on the rocks by the water, sat down and, before I knew it, Tim had slipped off his clothes and dived into the lake. He dared me to follow suit, a dangerous, teasing offer. At first, I was afraid that a policeman would drive by, sound his siren, and arrest the two of us. I could just see the headlines that my kids undoubtedly would read the next morning: "Man and Woman Arrested for Indecent Exposure." Yet I accepted his dare and swam out to meet him. The water was frigid and my feet were getting numb but I knew that if I got a leg cramp and started to go under, Tim would rescue me. And even if he couldn't, I didn't care. I didn't care about cops patrolling the beach or scandalous newspaper headlines or getting swallowed by a seiche. I didn't care much about anything that night, except being alive.

We made it back to shore without any police or cardiac arrests, quickly put our clothes on and sat on the rocks, looking at the lake. Haunted by images of my brother who was slipping away, I began to tremble. Tim held me for the longest time, without either of us saying a word. Was he taking advantage of my helplessness? Perhaps. But I realize now that my attraction to Tim was quite simple: he represented life. In the past few years, my mother had died, followed by my husband. I was surrounded by so much illness and death that I merely wanted to feel alive, once again. I wanted the profound pain to disappear, if only for one night. So, we went to my apartment, put on some soft music, had a few glasses of wine, and made love . . . this time without phone wires between us.

I received the call from the hospital at eight the next morning, about an hour after Tim had left. Three days later, Tim came to my brother's funeral. I was touched. He didn't know Tommy, and no one at the funeral knew Tim. I introduced him as my friend, because he was. For the rest of that year, Tim and I saw each other on and off—more off, actually—on an occasional Wednesday or Friday night. But not on Saturday and, as Melina Mecouri would say, never on Sunday. I knew why, but I didn't care. I needed someone to get me through the dark times. And Tim was, after all, "my man," as Marv had promised. My random, safe man.

It was fall of 1999. I immersed myself in my work, but pre-holiday loneliness was still getting the better of me. Although months had passed and we had talked far less frequently, I called Tim at the office one evening where I knew he'd be and asked him for a favor. That was the great thing about Tim and me—we could go for weeks without talking, yet we would pick up right where we had left off.

Tim said, "A favor? Just name it, Franny."

I asked him if he would accompany me to my annual black-tie benefit that I was overseeing at work . . . an event that I couldn't bear going to alone once again. Just a few years earlier, my husband was my "date." The following year, my brother was my escort. Now he, too, was gone. Tim asked me when the event was.

"Three weeks from Saturday," I said.

There was an uncomfortable silence, but then Tim answered, "Anything for you, Franny."

As the date of the affair approached, I was feeling relieved that I wouldn't have to attend it alone. It was primarily a working evening for me but, still, it was going to feel nice to have a companion by my side, a partner for that last dance, and someone to help me forget about the losses of the last several years.

It was the Tuesday evening before my Saturday benefit. Tim called me at home. He said that he had bad news. He was in Cleveland for a deposition and he said that based on the way the trial was going, he'd probably be stuck there for at least a week. He was sorry, but he wouldn't be able to accompany me to my event after all.

I knew—even before Tim called allegedly from Cleveland, while my caller ID (a new device that was just becoming popular in those days) showed him to be in Chicago—that my formal affair might be in four days but my informal, if infrequent, one was over. I knew that timing was everything. I needed somebody to get me through the rough post- and pre-funeral times. And Tim did just that. I needed someone to talk with late at night when I was feeling frightened, and Tim was that someone. I needed somebody to remind me that amidst all of this death there was life out there, and Tim was that reminder. For a brief time, Tim was there and he was my man . . . albeit a married one whose wife undoubtedly would have insisted on knowing where he was going in a tux on a Saturday night.

And that's how I connected with my acquaintance, Barry. Although I hadn't talked to Barry in years, I called him forty-eight hours before my benefit, having heard through the grapevine that he was going through his third divorce, and asked him if he'd like to attend my dinner dance. I apologized for the last-minute notice, explaining to him that I had had an escort who had just cancelled. Barry said, "Are you kidding me? I haven't been out on a date in fourteen years. What time should I pick you up?"

That was the beginning of nearly a year of some laughs with the over self-served Barry, a man who loved to cook, stirring up a mean meal with one hand while swigging from a Dasani water bottle with the other. What made his water bottle unique, however, was that it was filled with gin. I eventually discovered that Barry's routine cuisine was gin with a tiny splash of juice in the morning to accompany his bacon and eggs; gin for lunch, all by itself (he was trying to count calories); and gin in the evening with a good cut of meat, before turning in for the night. Watching his diet was beyond my comfort level.

I can best summarize the demise of my relationship with Barry by describing our last date. We were out for dinner at an old favorite restaurant of his—one that was unfamiliar to me. When the waitress approached our table to take our order and asked if she could start us off with a cocktail, Barry said, "Yes, two Bombay martinis with a twist." She started to walk away, undoubtedly assuming that one of the drinks was for me, when I called after her, "And I'll take a glass of Chardonnay." She looked confused, walked back to our table and repeated, "Two martinis with a twist and one glass of Chardonnay. Gotcha." When she turned around and headed over to the bar, Barry leaned toward me, lowered his voice, and whispered, "Trust me. I've been here quite a few times. The food is great, but the service is *really* slow."

And that, along with a little help from my friends, is what brought me online. I owe my takeoff into cyber world to the phases I was going through at the time. To touching base with a man who had experienced the loss of a lifetime partner: Joe, my former colleague with whom I no longer had much in common except widowhood. To leaning on someone who took care of all of the mundane but necessary details of life after death . . . reminding me that there *was* life after death: Tim, my attorney who helped me draw up one will and break down another. And finally, to looking for an occasional source of entertainment: Barry, an acquaintance whose amusing anecdotes helped to ease my pain for a while until it stopped being fun . . . until I realized that taking a chance on a total stranger might be stranger but couldn't be any emptier than spending my time with someone who spent so much of his in a fog. I have my three stages—Barry, Curly, and Joe—and my girlfriends to thank or blame for getting me online where I met my very first cyber date, Mr. Everyone-Is-Out-To-Get-Me Shelly, along with the many others whom you are about to meet.

5

Richard

AFTER MY INTERNET LAUNCH with Shelly, I felt different at work, as if everyone knew my secret cyber life and was snickering about it behind my back. Of course, they didn't and weren't. The only two people who knew about my new venture were Linda and Nancy. I couldn't even tell my older sister, Connie. Ever since we had lost our brother a year after Bob died, she hovered over me. We were the only siblings left, and we were hanging onto each other for dear life. Nor had I shared my latest escapade with my grown children, Laura and Mark. I had no idea—nor did I even want to imagine—how they'd react. So, as I sat in a quarterly board meeting the morning after, I looked around the conference room table, trying to imagine what each coworker's reaction to my new-found, clandestine hobby might be.

My secretary, sitting there taking minutes, was a woman in her sixties who wore conservative clothes and sensible shoes. She would be appalled. Our finance director would want to figure out the statistical odds of my finding a perfect match. Our legal counsel would insist on reviewing my every candidate's email overtures for loopholes. Our marketing director would develop a branding campaign with a great tag line. I could see it now. Francine: Miss

Match or Mismatch! Our personnel director, whose husband I had the displeasure of meeting once, was probably a secret online dater herself. And my boss's reaction? Clueless, as usual.

"Francine, what do you think about this campaign strategy?" I heard our chairman say. Oh, my God. I was so worried about the possibility of my revealed cyber identity that I hadn't heard one word that had been uttered since the meeting had begun.

"I'm sorry, Ted. I was reviewing last week's revenue figures in my head. Could you repeat the question?" I asked nervously. My heart was pounding. There goes my job, I said to myself. I'll be out on the street in a month, living in a cardboard box on lower Wacker Drive, with no food—just me and my laptop on the curb, perusing my online candidates. Serves me right.

"Francine, we were talking about the latest strategy to try to gain a larger share of the market. What are your thoughts on its potential success?" he repeated with one brow slightly raised.

I was so flustered that I don't even remember what my answer was, but it must have been satisfactory because Ted smiled and nodded and went on to the next item on the agenda.

Okay, I thought to myself. I *could* have been preoccupied with last week's revenue. It's happened in the past. But now I was sure that everyone was staring at me, even though I could see two of my colleagues shuffling through papers while a third was yawning and a fourth was pouring herself a cup of coffee. Classic paranoia. That's it. Now, I'm becoming paranoid. I'll have to put this down on my ever-growing list of things to talk to my therapist about when I see her next week.

I worked the remainder of the day with a vengeance, overcompensating, no doubt, for my morning meeting gaffe. I left work at seven, drove home, walked right into my kitchen, poured myself a glass of wine, and checked my answering machine. Two telemarketers and a message from my sister. I hadn't spoken to her for three days. Did she know what I was up to? No, of course not. How could she? I'll call her later, I thought. I needed some time to unwind.

I sat down at my computer, logged on, and immediately

found myself responding to Richard. Some things are too good to be true. Richard was a retired doctor who, in his spare time—of which he apparently had much—dabbled in the arts. This was a promising sign. My late brother, a physician with a host of hobbies, once warned me to beware of doctors who had no other interests outside of medicine.

"They make lousy conversationalists at cocktail parties," Tommy said. "Unless, of course, it's a party filled with fellow physicians, in which case the talk will flow like an intravenous drip, ranging from duodenal ulcers to the latest laparoscopic surgery to transient ischemic attacks. If you ever date a doc, Franny, make sure he's well-rounded."

Richard seemed to fill the bill. In his striking photo, he was sporting a ski cap. I later learned that Richard was a bald skier. We talked in cyberspace for about two weeks. I could tell that he was intelligent, although his spelling was atrocious. And except for a few risqué remarks, he seemed normal enough.

Richard lived in a suburb of Milwaukee and kept a studio apartment in Chicago. We made a date to meet at a museum, which was holding a reception for the opening of one of its exhibits. I was curious about his lifestyle. I knew what medical school demanded: years of grueling education; sleepless nights on-call at the hospital; ingesting hot and cold caffeine, sometimes simultaneously; and board exams—all for a career in medicine. Richard must have been in his mid-thirties when he finally finished his residency and started his practice; and here he was, already retired. I didn't get it.

I met Richard in the museum's foyer. He was as easy to pick out of the crowd as I'm sure I was, as well. Except for the ninety-year-old woman behind the coat check table, Richard and I were clearly the two oldest people in the place, each by about twenty years. Richard said that he was a member of this museum's volunteer youth group, so I figured he liked to hang out with younger people. Nothing wrong with that, I thought. I have close friends who range in age from twenty to eighty. Again, a well-rounded guy, I tried to tell myself.

"Francine?" he said, extending his hand.

"Richard," I answered.

Richard was a nice-looking man. Not as good looking as his photo, but perhaps it was air brushed. He was wearing black trousers, a black turtle neck, and a black sports coat. We looked as though we had consulted each other before leaving home, as I was wearing my always-appropriate black pants suit. Other than my pearls, we were dressed like twins.

"I was hoping you'd be showing some leg," Richard said, as his eyes traveled up and down my body. "I love it when my dates wear short skirts or dresses."

"Me, too," I replied, as my stomach started squeezing against my ribcage. He just looked at me quizzically. This was going to be one long night.

Richard took my arm and led me to one of several bars. While in line, he started to rub my back with his hand. His touch gave me a queasy chill, and I quickly pulled away from him. What next, I cynically thought? I'd better be on guard in case he pulls out a stethoscope and wants to listen to my lungs.

"What are you drinking, Francine?" he asked. For a moment I thought he had asked me what I was *thinking*, and I was certain that he wouldn't want to know.

"Chardonnay," I replied. Whenever I was nervous, I ordered white wine instead of red so that if I spilled it all over myself or my date, it wouldn't stain. This was definitely going to be a Chardonnay evening.

We walked around the museum and although Richard had said that he was a member of this auxiliary group, it seemed like he barely knew a soul except for a few young guys who acknowledged him with a wave from across the room. As we viewed the artwork, his arm kept going around my waist or my shoulder or he'd try to slip his hand in mine, and I just as quickly kept detaching myself from him. Finally I spotted an empty table, unfortunately in a dark corner of the room. But I needed a place to set my wine and hors d'oeuvres down and, besides, I felt better with a table between us, even if it was a secluded one.

"So tell me about your retirement, Richard. I'm envious of all your free time." This was my first fib of the evening. I genuinely enjoy my job and look forward to going to work every morning. Sure, there are days when I would like to roll over and sleep a few more hours. But I'm convinced that one of the reasons I rarely get ill is because back in 1998 when I had the flu for three days, I nearly lost my mind at home as I shuffled between the kitchen for ginger ale and the living room couch, where all the remote control could find was Maury Povich, Jerry Springer, and Regis and sidekick, each of whom entertained me for a maximum of about two minutes. But when you are burning up with a fever, your eyes are too watery to read, and the sound of music hurts your ears—and besides, you can't even stand up long enough to load the CD player—daytime television is the only alternative that reminds you that you are still alive.

"Well, I was a cosmetic surgeon, but about five years ago I broke my right hand in a skiing accident and it never healed properly. I tried to compensate by forcing myself to use my left hand more when I would operate, even though I'm right-handed. But, I finally had to give up my practice. You know, you need both of your hands to perform surgery," Richard replied.

I immediately pictured Quasimodo from *The Hunchback of Notre Dame* or the subject of a Modigliani painting with lopsided eyes and an off-center nose. I wondered who Richard's last plastic surgery patient was and what that person was doing now with the huge malpractice settlement that was undoubtedly awarded.

"Oh, how terrible," I said. "Especially after all of those years of medical school."

"Yeah, tell me about it. That's when I decided to go back to school to train in another specialty, one where using my hands wouldn't be a factor," he went on.

Good thinking, I said to myself.

"So I took a residency in pathology at the University of Wisconsin," he continued. "But after a year, I was bored to death, no pun intended.

"So, then what?" I asked, with a modicum of interest.

"So then I quit the path residency and decided to get out of medicine altogether," he replied.

"So *now* what do you do with your time?" my inquiring mind wanted to know.

"Well, I've penned two short stories, but neither has been published; and I play trombone in a band. I'm a member of the musicians union, which provides me with health insurance. And that's fortunate because I had to have an emergency appendectomy two months ago. I was pretty sick for a few weeks after the surgery. In fact, I had just started a new job at the time, but they let me go after I got ill. I guess they thought I really didn't need all of that time off. I've hired a great lawyer, though, who says I have a good chance of getting rehired. I hope he's right, because I loved that job."

"What job was that?" I asked.

"I was a counselor at an erectile dysfunction clinic. In fact, that's where I got the material for my stories. I hope someone will publish them some day. They're really interesting."

Dr. Strangelove alluded to being well-off. One of three children whose parents had died, he and each of his siblings had inherited a large trust fund. He was divorced twice, had no children. "None that I know of . . . heh, heh, heh." And he traveled a lot.

"I took a wonderful trip last month to Hong Kong," Richard continued. "I brought this fourteen-year-old boy who lives in a group home on the trip with me. I volunteer for an agency that places these kids in foster care. I've sort of taken him under my wing."

"Sounds fascinating," I said.

Richard then started asking me about my profession. I was vague about where I worked, following my gut, which was starting to ache. After dodging questions about my salary, when and where I lost my virginity, and what my wildest sexual fantasy was, I told Richard that I had an early morning meeting and needed to get home. I should have paid more attention to his suggestive email comments.

Richard went outside with me to help me find a cab so that I wouldn't have to walk to where I had parked my car. When I got into the taxi, I turned to say goodnight, only to find Richard in the back seat beside me. I had never been so happy to see such a large, burly-looking cabdriver in my life.

"Might as well share the ride with you. I was going to take a taxi back to my place anyway. But I'll drop you off at your car first. Unless, of course, you want to come up to my apartment for a nightcap. I could show you my etchings . . . heh, heh, heh," Richard laughed.

I hadn't heard that line since I had rented a Mae West and W.C. Fields movie.

"Driver, you can pull over here. My car is just down the block. No thanks, Richard. But thank you for a nice evening," I lied. "Goodnight," I said, as I jumped out of the taxi. And good-bye and good luck with your life, I thought.

I drove home feeling even more exhausted than I had after date number one. I walked into my apartment, filled the tub with bubbles, and stepped in with a glass of iced tea and the latest issue of *The New Yorker*. I read the movie reviews and then, while turning the pages, I came across an ad with a picture of a woman in it who struck a remarkable resemblance to a photo I had of my mother when she was in her twenties. As a young girl, I idolized my mother and wanted to grow up to be exactly like her. She was beautiful, had a sensuous figure, long brown hair, and sparkling brown eyes. She loved to talk and to laugh. She would graciously greet people on the street, whether or not she knew them. That always amazed me. And she coped.

Whatever life handed my mother, she accepted with aplomb. If she felt down about something, she pulled herself up when she thought of those who were less fortunate. And she assured us that she personally knew many such people. After several years of therapy, I learned that her way of dealing with life's challenges was not healthy. I later was told that I should have questioned her coping mechanism and her lack of sympathy toward herself. Experts tried to convince me that she was in denial of the various hardships and disappointments that she had experienced during her life. But to this day, I don't know what was so bad about the way that she dealt with difficulties. She seemed happy. She was productive. She truly cared about people. And her legacy of coping had worked well for me.

I slid down further into the warm bubbles as I thought about the awful date with Richard. My mother was right once again. She always said, "When things seem too good to be true, they usually are."

I pinched my nose and submerged my face under water like I did when I was a kid. As I came up for air, I blurted aloud, "Okay, Mom, you were right this time. But your daughter's coping. And she's not giving up."

Giving up wasn't an option when we were young. I recalled the time I was having trouble with calculus and wanted to switch to an easier course that would fulfill the mathematics requirement and help me glide right into graduation. "Don't even consider it," warned my mother. "Your sister will be home from school this weekend, and she'll be happy to help you." In our house, we started what we finished. Sometimes a chess board would sit for days with a sign on it that read, "Do not move. Game in progress." When I was thirteen, I wanted to take violin lessons. From the first time I slid the bow over the strings, I knew that it was hopeless. But my parents had invested in a teacher, sheet music, a rented instrument, and most likely earplugs. So I hung in there for a year. Perseverance ruled.

That same persistence followed me into my marriage, as I juggled two small children during the day while taking classes at night to finish college. One evening, I called my brother, who had recently started his own family. I told him that I no longer could do it all. Being a stay-at-home mom, studying by day, getting dinner on the table by night, changing the parental guard with Bob when he got home from work so that I could run to class. It was getting to be too much. Tommy's advice was to follow my heart and do what I most wanted to do.

I had learned early on in my marriage that what I cherished most was being at home with my children: two little people, over whom I had such enormous influence. Every minute with them was a wonder. Every day they made me laugh. But I also wanted to pursue my dream of getting my degree so that when my own children were off to school, I could begin teaching others.

It was tough. There were days when I went from reading Shakespeare's *Hamlet* in preparation for final exams as I was pouring Fruit Loops into breakfast bowls, to reciting Dr. Seuss' *Green Eggs and Ham* to the kids' squeals of laughter . . . from cutting out paper dolls with my daughter and watching *Sesame Street* with my son, while scribbling an outline for a term paper on the inside cover of an old coloring book. And there were nights when I thought I'd barely be able to stay awake in class, let alone behind the wheel of the car as I drove home. But I stuck with it. And I'll never forget the looks on the faces of my husband, my children, and especially my parents, or the sound of their cheers coming from the audience when I crossed the stage to get my college diploma. I persevered.

Was this *learned* behavior now coming back to haunt me in my cyber search? The relentless determination was beginning to feel familiar.

6

Frank

ALTHOUGH I NEVER THOUGHT that I would consider dating someone who was still officially married, here I was, making a date with Frank. At least he was up front about his marital status.

Frank's introductory email said that he had separated two years prior to joining the world of Internet dating. He went on to say that he and his wife parted quite amicably. Now, I'm a bit cynical about those friendly splits. In my experience, albeit limited, there's usually a fairly serious reason why two people break up. A gambling problem. Refusal to work. Physical abuse. Emotional starvation. Another love interest. An addiction. Nonetheless, I was not about to be judgmental of Frank's soon-to-be split, which, he assured me, *was* soon to be.

Frank said that he expected his divorce to be final in about eight weeks, and that he was "emotionally healthy and ready to enter into another partnership." That phrase was a little perplexing. I wanted to get to know him over a cup of coffee, not draw up a legal agreement.

Frank was a writer. Well, writing was his hobby. His day job was managing a small public relations firm. He had written many short stories and was waiting for one of them to be published. I felt that at least we had this interest in common as I'd had a short story appear in a magazine a few years earlier.

We made arrangements to meet for dinner at a local, casual place. It was easy to recognize Frank when he walked in as he looked just like his picture. Not very good, but that was alright. Handsome wasn't a top priority of mine.

"Francine?" he asked

"Frank," I confirmed.

"What a coincidence," Frank said. "I've been thinking about this since our last email, the one where you revealed your real first name: Francine . . . you're Francine. Frank . . . I'm Frank. Francine. Frank. Alliteration. Get it? I take this as a sign," he said.

I take this as a nut, I thought.

"So, what *is* your sign, if I may ask?" Frank continued.

"My what?"

"Your sign. You know, astrologically speaking. Your zodiac sign?"

"Oh, let's see. I'm an Aries," I said.

"That explains it," he exclaimed.

"Explains what?"

"You arrived at the restaurant first. Aries is the first sign of the zodiac. No wonder."

Oh, right. Why hadn't I thought of that? I immediately recalled one of my first days of teaching high school many years ago. As I was introducing the syllabus to my new students and laying out my expectations of them, one girl raised her hand and asked me what my sign was. When I answered "Aries," she stood up, gathered her books and said, "I knew it. I'm out of here." I never saw her again. I later learned that she had transferred into another class, taught by a Pisces or Leo or Sagittarius, no doubt. Until then, I had no idea that people took astrology so seriously.

"I'm a Libra," Frank continued. "It's the seventh sign of the zodiac. My nickname, 'Frankie,' has seven letters in it. The word 'library,' which coincidentally has seven letters in it, is a derivative of 'libra.' 'Libra' also translates to 'book' in Latin and several other foreign languages. Get it? I'm a writer. I'm working on a book. I'm a Libra."

How do you say fruitcake in Spanish, I thought to myself?

"Well, shall we look at a menu?" I asked.

"Shall we. Very good. Not should we . . . 'shall' with first person singular or plural," Frank went on.

I wondered if this was how Hemingway or Steinbeck got started. Did they recite the parts of speech and point out correct and incorrect grammar to each other and their peers? Or were they too busy drinking and writing?

"Well, I guess I should always know better, Frank. I'm a former English and journalism teacher, you know."

"Always should know."

"Know what?"

"No, 'always should know' better. 'Should always know' better is a split infinitive."

"You're right, Frank. Let's order."

"How hungry are you, Francine?"

"I'm seldom very hungry," I said carefully. Two adverbs and an adjective. Was that allowed, I wondered?

"Well, in that case, maybe we should split something," he went on.

"We just did," I said.

"Did what?"

"We just did," I repeated. "The infinitive—we split it," I chuckled.

Frank just looked at me.

"I think I will simply order my own salad. Wait. Allow me to correct myself. I think I simply shall order my own salad. How's that? No splits of any kind in that sentence," I said.

By this time, the waitress had been standing at our table for at least a minute, listening to our high school Grammar 101 exchange.

"One house salad for the lady. And for you, sir?" she asked.

"I'd like a grilled cheese sandwich and a chocolate milk."

Now I truly felt like I was back in high school—the cafeteria, in particular.

While waiting for our food, Frank pulled out two sheets of paper that were stapled together. For a minute I thought that he was going to capture the moment and begin writing. Instead, he started to review my Internet profile, which he obviously had printed.

"Hey, what happened to the curly hair?" he asked me. "In this picture, you have curly hair. I like curly hair."

"It was raining the day the picture was taken, Frank. When it rains, my hair gets curly. The air is very dry today, so it's straight. Bipolar manes are not uncommon. Sorry," I replied. And what happened to your locks, Frank? When did they vanish altogether, I thought to myself?

When the waitress brought us our food, I surreptitiously glanced at my watch. We had met at six-thirty. It was now six-fifty. The last twenty minutes seemed like two hours—about the average length of an English class.

"So, you have a daughter who lives in Portland, huh? I've been to Portland many times. I had a client out there," Frank said.

"I have a daughter, but she doesn't live in Portland. She lives in Chicago," I replied, somewhat confused.

"No, you said she lived in Portland," Frank insisted.

"Frank, I think I know where my own daughter lives. She lives right here in Chicago." This was getting tedious.

"Wait a minute," Frank went on, as he glanced at my printed profile. "I think I stapled the wrong second page to your first."

Instead of being insulted that he had me half confused with another Internet sweetie, I was finding this perversely amusing.

"So, what are you writing these days, Frank?" I asked. Let him do all of the talking, I thought, so I could check his subject/verb agreement.

"I'm writing a novel," he said in a whisper.

"A novel. That's impressive. How much have you written?"

"Well, I really don't know. You see, I have all of these short stories that I've written over the years, and what I plan on doing is taking them—these short stories—and putting them all together into a longer novel," he said, very seriously.

"Gee, I didn't know that was the creative process. You mean *Grapes of Wrath* started out as *A Raisin in the Sun*?" I joked.

"I'm serious, Francine. I mean I have the theme and everything."

"Oh? What's the theme?"

"I hesitate telling anyone for fear that someone might steal my idea," Frank said in a barely audible tone.

"You don't have to tell me if you don't want to, Frank. But I can assure you that I will divulge the theme to no one."

"Okay. I'll tell you the title of my novel. I'm calling it '*More Than Solitude*.' It's about a man who's looking for solitude. He eventually finds it and a whole lot more. Get it? *More* than solitude."

Frank went on and on about how he had already begun to cut and paste the various short stories that he had written over the years, building them into one, long novel. I was getting confused just imagining it.

"I have 14,240 words so far. That's about fifty pages. I figure I'm about a quarter of the way done with it."

"Finished," I said.

"No, I'm not finished yet."

"No, you're about a quarter of the way 'finished,' not a quarter of the way 'done,'" I teased.

"Hey, you're good. You could be my editor. Really, I mean it. Would you consider editing these stories for me? You'd have your name in the book, *More Than Solitude*."

"I don't think so, Frank. I'm pretty busy. But thanks for the offer. I've got to get home now. I have a huge day tomorrow. Let's split the check," I said as I took a ten dollar bill out of my wallet, put it on the table, stood up, and extended my hand.

"Can we do this again sometime? I mean *may* we?" Frank asked.

Now, this is where I have a hard time. It's so difficult for me simply to say "thanks but no thanks." When I feel sorry for someone, it can get me into trouble. And I was starting to feel a little sorry for Frank who, I think, was probably a genuinely nice man. Just not the man for me. It was awkward, but I had to find my voice sooner rather than later.

"I don't think so, Frank. I'm a busy girl. And it sounds like you're a busy guy, what with your novel being a quarter finished and all. But thanks for a nice evening. I'll always remember it," I said sincerely.

I left the restaurant and walked to my car. I couldn't wait to get home and take a bubble bath. I was tired. I had had a long day at work. And I didn't want to talk to anyone for the rest of the night. I was yearning for some solitude. No, not just some . . . even *more* than solitude.

Solitude, I thought to myself as I was driving home, isn't all bad. It's strange. I had felt just the opposite most of my life. Probably because I knew nothing else. I had gone from my parents' home to college interrupted to marriage and raising children for three decades and, now, to widowhood. What was it like being alone? For years, I really didn't know. The day Bob died, my sister must have seen the look of terror on my face because she simply said, "Don't worry. I'll stay with you tonight," which turned into five. On night six, I moved Bob's memorial candle into the bedroom, where his spirit remained long after the flame was gone.

The day of his death will be etched into my brain forever. In fact, for almost a year, that dreadful day overshadowed the preceding thirty years of marriage. It was the same with my father, who was in a coma for seven months before he quietly stopped breathing; with my mother, who really didn't know us for the last ten weeks of her life; and with my brother, whose final twelve days were spent in a semiconscious state in a hospital bed. It was that one day, those seven months, the ten weeks, and those last dozen days that I couldn't get out of my mind. For months, I saw my mother's vacant stare, my father's mouth grimacing, my brother's jaundiced face, Bob's body being placed in a bag, zipped up, and shipped off to the funeral home—and nothing else. I would drag out photo albums to help me remember romantic vacations in Aruba; Father's Day barbecues in our backyard; mother-daughter

birthday teas at the Drake Hotel; my brother and I trading wise-
cracks at the dinner table. Then I'd place the pictures back on the
closet shelf, and the dying bodies and corpses would return.

It was the July curse. All of these deaths, save my father's, took
place in July. In July of 1995, my mother died. In July of 1997,
my husband. In July of 1998, my brother. For the next few years,
I'd flip my wall calendar from June to August, so petrified was
I to turn to that dreaded page. I started taking my vacations in
July, hoping that being in another city or country would erase
these memories of death. If I was walking around on the island of
Hydra, maybe the funerals would diminish in my mind. If I was
shopping for silver or embroidered linen in Ixtapa, maybe I could
forget the pain of seeing bodies in caskets. I was wrong. These
memories haunted me for several years. Then, miraculously, they
slowly began to fade and were replaced with the selected memories that I so dearly cherished.

Memories of my father teaching me to dance by letting me
stand atop his shoes so that I felt like I was gliding along with
Gene Kelly. Memories of my mother in an evening gown that
she donned for our church's annual black-tie dinner dance and
twirled around in, at my insistence, while I pretended that there
was a queen in our very own living room. Memories of my brother convincing me that nothing bad would happen if I did not turn
my light switch on and off twice before I went to bed, a super-
stitious ritual that took hold when I was about seven and that I
thankfully outgrew a few months later. And memories—far too
many—of Bob: our first night together in a motel on the outskirts
of Madison; his resilience and endurance while teaching me how
to drive; our taking turns sitting up all night with a croupy child
in a steamy bathroom, terrified as we watched wallpaper peel off
the walls from the humidity; his arm tight around my shoulder
as we waved good-bye to our daughter on her very first day of
school; his patience, years later, when I made him drive around
the block seven times after dropping her off as a freshman at her
college dorm; and, most of all, his infectious sense of humor that
could tickle even the biggest prude and coax belly laughs out of

children everywhere. These were the memories that would keep me company on cold, lonely evenings. These were the memories that would get me through life's bumps.

I was beginning to realize that these were also the memories that I wanted to store away in a safe place while creating new ones with another. And this realization was most unsettling.

7

Jack

As I reviewed cyber profiles and photos over the next few months, I made a disturbing discovery: My standards were beginning to slide. I was becoming weary of wading through dozens and dozens of candidates' emails, only to discover a paltry few who had good match potential. Note that I'm not equating match potential with long-term relationship, although that may have been an objective at the onset of my search. I am merely talking about someone with whom I even would like to match up over a cup of coffee or a glass of wine.

Onward.

Do you like black leather jackets and gold chains? Do you like Borscht Belt comedy? Then you're going to love Jack.

Although Jack's profile was very brief, it seemed interesting. Jack lived within a few miles of me, was an avid jogger, and had a job. I had stopped caring about what type of profession these candidates were in—salesman, teacher, musician, waiter, chef, drug-runner—if they worked at all, I considered it a good sign. Jack was divorced and had two teenaged children. His posted photo showed an ordinary-looking guy with light brown hair and brown eyes. The photo, I soon would discover, was at least ten years old. Either that, or he had gained a pound for each strand of hair he had lost between the Monday when we began emailing one another and the following Thursday when we met.

The one thing that was most attractive to me about Jack's profile was his self-proclaimed wit. All through my life, humor was essential. The subtle, spontaneous, intellectual kind. The off-center, unrestrained variety, too. One of my fondest childhood memories of my parents was sitting between them on the couch in our living room and seeing them laugh till they cried as they watched *The Jack Benny Show*. My parents lived through the Great Depression. They had seen more sorrow than I thought, albeit mistakenly, I ever would experience in my lifetime. And, still, they could laugh.

Then along came my husband's outrageous sense of humor. Anyone who could respond to the Target employee's question of "May I help you?" with "No thanks, we're just here for the music," as he then took me in his arms and started dancing down the small appliances aisle, won my heart forever.

Jack and I didn't email each other much. In retrospect, perhaps that was a mistake, although I thought that I was beginning to learn how to cut through the rhetoric. After all, shouldn't one exchange reveal enough about a candidate? When Jack wrote that he had a great sense of humor and was looking for the same, I didn't hesitate accepting a date. We met at the now-ubiquitous book-store-with-coffee-bar. I had difficulty recognizing him, as he truly had lost most of his hair and found about fifty pounds since the picture of him that I had viewed just four days prior. I was sitting with a cup of coffee, reading the best sellers' reviews, when a pleasant looking, round-faced, balding man came up to me and said, "Are you Francine?"

"Jack?" I replied, extending my hand.

He sat down at the table and slipped off his black leather jacket, revealing a shirt that was unbuttoned half-way down his chest and two gold, rope-like chains dangling around his neck. Okay, fashion can be developed, I thought to myself.

"Have you been waiting long?" he asked.

"No, I just got here," I lied. My Type A personality had over-estimated traffic and I actually had been sitting in the bookstore for about a half hour, but I didn't want to appear too anxious. It's funny how you analyze your every move on these first dates.

We exchanged preliminary comments about the general areas where we each lived, being careful not to be too specific in case one of us turned out to be a stalker. Then we began talking about what brought us to Internet dating.

"I've been a widow for the past five years," I said. "And I just haven't met many quality men who share common interests with me—including my most recent relationship. How about you?"

"Well, I was married for twenty-two years, but I'm divorced now," Jack replied. "My marriage ended one day at about three in the morning. My wife and I were asleep when the phone rang. She answered it and said, 'How should I know? That's about 800 miles from here,' and then she hung up. When I asked her who was on the phone, she said 'I don't know . . . some woman wanting to know if the coast was clear.'" And with that, Jack started to guffaw.

At first, I just sat there. "Oh, I get it. That's a joke," I said, forcing a smile.

"I mean, my wife was always telling me that I should be more affectionate. So I got *two* girlfriends."

Bada Bing.

"So where do you work?" Jack asked me.

"I work in a medical center. I head up the fundraising department."

"Do you interact with doctors much?"

"Occasionally, if I need their input for a proposal or something like that," I replied.

"You know, funny thing about doctors. You wait a month and a half to get an appointment to see them and then, when you finally do, they shake their heads and say, 'I wish you had come to see me sooner.' Ha, ha, ha," he said, slapping his thigh.

This time, I ignored his response and just continued, "So how long have you been divorced, Jack?"

"About two years. It took me awhile to get used to being single again. I was a little depressed at first, but I got through it. You know what I start to do whenever I feel blue?" he asked.

"No, what?" I asked, with some trepidation.

"I start breathing again. Ha, ha, ha, ha, ha."

The muscles in my face were beginning to tighten, as I tried to smile.

"No, seriously," he continued. "I tried to be faithful to my wife. But it's not easy. Did you know that eighty percent of married men cheat in America? The rest cheat in Europe."

Bada Boom.

"So what do you do for fun, Jack?" I continued. And please give me a straight answer or I'm going to reach over this table and grab you by the throat, I thought to myself.

"Well, I like to go out to eat. There are so many great restaurants in Chicago. Just the other night, I was at this nice little family-type restaurant. I could tell that it was a family place because at every table there was an argument going on. Ha, ha."

About ten minutes had crawled by. Ever the optimist, I blamed his Henny Youngman routine on first-encounter jitters, as I foolishly continued the conversation.

"So, Jack, how old are your kids?"

"They're both teenagers. I told them that they at least have to finish high school, even if they already know everything. Seriously, I never finished college, and I regret it. I had to drop out and help support my folks. But that was years ago, and times have changed. How old do you think I am?" he asked, obviously forgetting that he had listed his age on his Internet profile.

Did I dare reply?

"I'd guess you to be about fifty," I said kindly. Although your material is closer to a hundred, I thought to myself.

"You're very close. Actually, I'm $49.95, plus shipping and handling. Ha, Ha, Ha, Ha, Ha."

His sit-down comedy routine was starting to make my head hurt.

"Listen, Jack, this has been nice, but I have a big day tomorrow at work, so I'd better finish my coffee and get home," I said, as I chugged my decaf.

"Okay. Must be interesting working in a hospital. You know, all of those health nuts are gonna feel stupid someday, lying in hospitals dying of nothing. Ha, Ha, Ha."

With that, I got up and extended my hand to shake his, although I fully expected a buzzer to go off in his palm.

"I've gotta go. Good-bye, Jack." I suddenly could hear the Ray Charles' Raylettes in the background singing, "And don't cha come back no more, no more, no more, no more."

"Listen, Francine, I don't have your number, but you've got mine. Will you give me a ring sometime? Not a wedding band or anything like that. I mean, we don't know each other well enough yet. Maybe just a friendship ring. Ha, ha, ha, ha, ha."

Feeling ill, I forced a smile and waved good-bye as I ran out of the bookstore. I wanted to go home and reread *Crime and Punishment* or stop at Blockbusters and rent *Sophie's Choice*. I wanted to listen to sobering stories of murder and mayhem on the ten-o-clock news. I wanted *never* to hear another goddamned joke again as long as I lived.

Perhaps it was time to reprioritize my list of candidates' qualities. Maybe a sense of humor could come down a notch or two. After all, I would never stop seeing humor in almost everything. And I could always depend on *myself* to make me laugh, right?

In fact, I was beginning to understand that many of the qualities that I was looking for—the ones that I so deeply missed in my loved ones—were part of my own personality. This made perfect sense. Although opposites can attract, people usually seek out those who reflect most, if not all, of their own values and standards, likes and dislikes. At least this certainly was true of the people who were dear to me and were now gone.

My values were my parents'. I couldn't go to someone's home—whether it was for a cup of coffee or a five-course dinner—without bringing a small token of my appreciation. That was my father's hand-me-down standard. I learned from him the worth of hard work and how it was the common denominator of all people, as he opened our modest home at Christmas to the busboys, dishwashers, cooks, and wait staff, along with their families, who worked for him at the club that he managed for thirty-five years. I inherited my emotional nature from my mother, who could not get through an episode of *The Loretta Young Show* without breaking down over some doleful dilemma of Loretta's heroine of the week. If my father happened to be home during prime time, which was seldom with his twelve-hour workday, he would say, "Mother, it's only a television program," as he handed her his handkerchief. I caught my brother's joie de vivre. As the youngest sibling, I was his ever-ready accomplice, always willing to help short-sheet a bed; "misplace" our mother's Sunbeam ten-cup coffee percolator, her most prized appliance; or hide behind the couch with a tape recorder when our sister's boyfriend came to visit her.

I had been thinking about my late brother a lot these days. Although he was ten years older than I, he had a youthful aura about him that served as a magnet to people of all ages. Later on as an adult, I used to jokingly say that when I grew up I wanted to be as young as he.

I missed them all . . . my father and these July angels.

8

Brian

Meeting these Internet daters kicked up memories of my youth. Perhaps it was because there was a very small period—only six years—of dating in my past. It was a time that I never thought would return—one that I hoped I'd never have to revisit. Yet after three decades of couplehood, here was dating again, right in my face.

If nothing else, it was an education. I was learning quite a bit about men, something I hadn't had to bother with for many years. And I was discovering a great deal about myself, too, which was revealing.

Men are an interesting breed. Some want arm candy. A runway model to boost their egos. It doesn't matter if she has rice pudding for brains. It's the carton that's important. A few men—too few and too seldom, unfortunately—want an intellectual challenge. These men are usually very smart themselves and are not intimidated by a brainy partner. Other men need constant adulation. I know a few professors and trial attorneys who fall into this category. They want a captive audience. Now, I don't want to hear from the National Society of Educators or the ABA. I'm simply relating my experiences. Then, there is the category of grown men who are looking for their mothers. Enter Brian.

I didn't find Brian's profile on the Internet. He found mine. Perhaps that's because I hadn't been searching in the teen section. Alright, that's a bit hyperbolic. Brian wasn't eighteen, but he *was* eighteen years my junior. And his initial email came on so strong that, of course, my curiosity was piqued. Anyone's would be.

I was on the Internet one evening when that little red flag on my mailbox was hoisted on high. Perhaps this is the one, I thought. When you join the world of Internet dating, you *always* think that. Never mind that it's usually junk mail, an email from your boss, one of those interminable jokes, or sometimes a combination of all three. You never lose hope that it's an email from your future soul mate.

Brian's email started out like this:

"I keep reading and rereading your profile. I can tell that YOU are a very strong, intelligent, warm, and empathic individual! Which is why I am contacting YOU! These qualities sometimes put people off. Not me. If I wanted wishy-washy, I would never have emailed YOU! Your picture and profile say more about YOU than YOU will ever know! I would like to meet YOU soon! How about tomorrow night?"

Whoa, there. First of all, anyone who knows me, even casually, knows that I'm not impulsive. I am cautious to a fault. I don't make decisions hurriedly. I analyze a situation, sometimes ad nauseam, close friends have remarked. And those very same friends know something else about me: I seldom use exclamation points. Not to mention that seeing myself referenced in all capital letters was somewhat startling. Nonetheless, I visited Brian's profile to learn a little more about HIM!

Brian was in his thirties (I admit I was flattered), had been married once to a woman his age, and had no children. Their marriage broke up after two years. He had been in another relationship for about a year, ended it six months earlier, and was ready to date again. He had an MBA from the University of Minnesota and worked for a large corporation in the city. His photo looked like the actor/director Ron Howard with hair, taken about twenty years ago. In other words, Brian was very cute.

Despite my recent vow to cut to the cyber chase, I wanted to find out a little more about Brian before agreeing to meet him. Like if he had a curfew. So, I emailed him and asked him to elaborate on his profile, particularly about his work and his hobbies.

He answered my email and told me that he was the assistant director of marketing for an ad agency in the Loop. For fun, he liked movies, concerts, and sports. He belonged to a volleyball league that played once a week, which he thoroughly enjoyed.

Although I hadn't lobbed a volleyball since I had been forced to play in high school, I love music and movies. Let's give Opie a try, I said to myself. I just hope I don't end up feeling like Aunt Bee.

Brian and I agreed to meet after work for a drink. I decided there'd be no more meals. Too many restaurants have slow service, which can prove painful when meeting someone for the first time. A drink, on the other hand, can be slowly sipped or thrown back. So, a drink it was. Now, we needed to come up with a place.

"How about Willie's Bar downtown? It's pretty cool," Brian suggested.

Okay. What was I expecting? The Ritz or Four Seasons?

"You're on. Thursday evening at seven at Willie's," I replied.

I had never been to Willie's in my life. But I knew a friend of my niece's who tended bar there. A nice kid in his twenties who was putting himself through school.

On Wednesday evening, I was checking my email, when I received a greeting card. It was the cartoon character, Ziggy, with little hearts floating around his head. The caption read, "Can't wait to meet YOU!" For a second, I had the urge to print the email and hang it on my refrigerator door, next to my grandnephew's finger painting.

Fortunately on the Thursday in question, I didn't have any important meetings at work, so I dressed down: a pair of pants and a sweater. I didn't want to arrive at Willie's Bar looking like I was an inspector from the Board of Health. Although Brian undoubtedly would be coming straight from work in a coat and tie, I had an eighteen-year gap to fill. And I wanted to look like I had just stepped out of a Gap.

I arrived at the restaurant early and waved to my niece's friend, who didn't seem to remember me, thank God. I took a seat in a booth in the back of the place, keeping an eye out for Brian. Anonymity is what I preferred when I was out on these Internet dates, in case I ran into someone I knew . . . like my kids, who probably would have had quite a bit in common with Brian. In fact, the thought occurred to me that maybe he was a friend of theirs.

In less than five minutes, in walked Brian. He had a broad grin on his face, as the hostess ushered him to my table. He looked a lot taller than his picture—and a lot younger. I wanted to ask him for identification, but I figured I'd leave that to the server.

"Hi, Brian. I'm Francine," I said as I extended my hand.

"Hi, Francine," he said, as he leaned over and kissed me on the cheek.

Now, I'm a first generation American who is accustomed to all of my Mediterranean relatives kissing not one, but both of my cheeks, sometimes even pinching them—my face, that is—when we meet. So why was I a little nonplussed? This was, after all, another generation, I reminded myself.

"How are you, Brian, and how was your day?"

"I'll answer in a sec. What are you having? I'll just go get our drinks from the bar myself. I gotta have a brewski," he said.

For a minute I thought he was speaking Russian.

"Oh, I'll have a Chardonnay," I replied. Something vintage . . . 1950, perhaps, I thought to myself.

"Okay, back at you in a minute."

I tried to remember if I had taken my vitamins that morning. I felt like I was going to need them.

Brian returned with a Budweiser and a Chardonnay. He handed me my glass and clinked it with his bottle as he said, "Here's to you."

"Back at *you*," I said, instantly feeling like a total moron. In fact, I was thinking of stopping at Barnes & Noble on my way home to see if they had *The Complete Idiot's Guide to Dating an Adolescent.*

"So, how was your day?" I repeated.

"Great. My boss was out of town. So, I really caught a break today. Not that I don't work hard on my own, but it's nice not to have someone breathing down my neck all day, you know what I mean?"

"Sure do," I lied. I couldn't remember when I last had a boss looking over my shoulder. But then, again, that's probably a privilege you attain when you've been a member of the work force for a hundred years. Either that or I was getting Alzheimer's.

"So, Brian, do you have any plans for the weekend?"

"Yep. Me and some buddies are going to the Cubs game on Saturday afternoon and then we're going over to Blues & News afterwards. They have this great group performing there on weekends. 'Mental Floss' is their name. Ever hear of them?"

"No, I don't think so. What kind of music do they play?" I asked, further exposing my years.

"New age. Do you like new age?" he asked.

I didn't want to answer any questions with the word "age" in it.

"Sure, it's neat," I fibbed again. First of all, I don't remember when I last described anything as "neat" . . . except perhaps many years ago when I was extolling the virtues of cleanliness to my young children, pointing out to them that dust balls under their beds were not considered decorating accessories. And secondly, I don't have a clue what new age is, unless it's your next birthday. Same thing with hip-hop and heavy metal, the latter of which I always thought was a solid piece of expensive jewelry. I *do*, however, know what rap is, and I hate it.

"How about you, Francine. What are your weekend plans?"

Oh, I think I'll knit myself an afghan, I mused.

"I'm going to try to get over to the Art Institute to catch that new photo exhibit. Maybe take in a movie afterwards. I want to see the new French film with Catherine Deneuve."

That did it. Catherine Deneuve. "Who was *she*?" he was thinking.

"How can you stand subtitles?" Brian asked in utter amazement. "I mean, if I wanted to read, I'd stay home with a good book or *People* magazine or something."

It was a genuine question, without a trace of criticism. Similar to a question one of my children asked me once when they were very young: "Mommy, did you *mean* for your hair to turn out like that?" after I'd returned from the beauty shop. Just an innocent question.

I couldn't be rude to this boy, so we talked for about another half hour. He loved cars. He subscribed to *Car and Driver*. I didn't have the heart to tell him that I was driving a fourteen-year-old Toyota with 193,000 miles on it, and that no matter how hard I tried, I would never fully understand what rack and pinion steering was. He was a Bears fan whose dream was to have season tickets someday. I didn't want to mention that I had been a season ticket holder for almost as long as he was alive. His favorite television show was *Friends*. I was embarrassed to admit to him that I was probably the only American who had never made it through an entire episode.

I learned that he was an only child. That both of his parents had been killed in a car accident when he was in his late twenties, just months before his wedding. That he had thought about postponing the wedding, but his fiancé had all of the plans in place. That after their marriage ended, she moved back to her native Colorado.

I wanted to take this kid in my arms and hug him for all of his naïveté and loneliness. Sitting here, feeling like a housemother with one of her fraternity sons, I was flattered that he saw something attractive in my profile. I could have taken it further. But this was not about my ego. This was about my comfort level . . . and about a confused, lonely kid.

"You know, Brian, you're really cute. And somewhere out there is a girl—a young woman—your age who's your perfect match. There's someone out there for everyone. I really believe that. That's why I'm still hanging in there, after months of Internet courtship."

Courtship. Now there's a word that I'd bet Brian hadn't heard since he was forced to read *The Scarlet Letter* in high school. I stood up and started to offer my hand, but leaned over and gave Brian a kiss on the cheek instead, as I picked up the check.

"Tonight's on me, Brian. I've got to run. I have a huge meeting tomorrow morning. And my boss is not out of town, so I have to be on my best behavior. You know, you're going to make some lucky girl very happy. Like the one who's sitting at the end of the bar all by herself." I gestured to a young woman sipping a Perrier with a slice of lemon, pretending to be engrossed in the newspaper.

"She looks sweet—and kind of lonesome. And she's awfully pretty. Who knows? Maybe she's the one. Well, I have to get going. Good-bye, Brian. And good luck."

I paid the hostess and walked toward the front door of the restaurant. I couldn't help but smile as I looked back and saw Brian heading over to the girl at the bar. That a boy, Brian.

As I drove home, I realized that this Internet adventure was becoming much more than a way to meet men. It was a confidence builder. It was about discovering who I was. It was about reaffirming what I wanted and what I didn't want. I wanted a man who had encountered some of the same life experiences that I had. Not necessarily all of them, but a person who could relate to bygone eras, music of the fifties and sixties, old movies, parenting trials. And speaking as a parent with two grown children of her own, I definitely didn't want another kid, albeit a darling one.

I suddenly remembered that I hadn't spoken to either of mine for almost two weeks. I was trying to walk that fine line between always being there for them and letting go. I definitely preferred the former, especially as I seemed to have a lot of time in my life lately. Theirs, on the other hand, were full and forward looking, as they should be. I quickly checked in with each of them when I returned home from my date with Brian.

First, my son, as I knew that our conversation would be brief.

How was his work going? The new house? When could we get together? Give my love to the family.

Next was my daughter. These were always longer conversations. Had she seen the latest George Clooney movie? Wasn't he a babe? What was I wearing to my niece's wedding? Would black shoes go with a turquoise dress or would bone be better? Who was I going to vote for in the upcoming election? Would I be interested in going with her and some friends to the Diana Krall concert?

I hung up the phone and recalled how much I loved being needed and how terribly I missed it. But I also knew in my heart that need wasn't the basis for a healthy, grown-up relationship. And I was, at the very least, all grown up. Although I certainly was feeling very young tonight.

9

Paul

Instead of discouraging me forever, my date with Brian was energizing. I was ready to scroll on . . . to Paul.

Paul was short. Not the man, the date. Actually it was one of my longer dates in hours and minutes, but it was brief in substance. I'm still puzzled about the outcome. I liked Paul.

Paul and I exchanged emails for about a week. His were thoughtful, refreshingly well-written, and intelligent. He said that he'd been unattached for about fifteen years, which was encouraging. The men who were on the rebound as they were leaving divorce court or the cemetery were far too numerous, and although I knew how those scenarios were going to end, I was ready to play them out anyway. After all, you're advised to give everyone a fair chance. So, in the beginning, that's what I did. If I didn't particularly care for someone's looks in their posted photo, as long as their emails sounded decent and they wanted to meet, I was ready. Maybe aviator glasses would make a comeback someday. If they had trouble spelling, I gave them a pass. Even Shakespeare had an editor. If the ink was barely dry on their settlement papers, I still was willing to risk—horror of horrors—being their transitional woman. Why? Because, I was learning that in Internet dating, just as in life, you need to take chances.

Paul was a sports enthusiast. At least one sport: golf. His cyber name was "Nicklaus Wannabe." His Internet picture was of himself on the course, leaning on his club. Quite Arnold Palmerish, I thought. A cross between preppy and country club casual. He said that he loved to play every chance that he could—golf, that is—but because he worked full time as a CFO of a mid-sized company, unless he was sealing a deal with a client who golfed, he didn't get out on the course much except on weekends. This kind of put a damper on his Internet social life, as he was never quite sure what time he'd be getting off the course to don his dating attire and be ready to meet a fellow Internetter.

Okay, I was getting the hint. Did I play golf? The answer was somewhat. Did I want to play golf on Saturday? Well, although it certainly wasn't my first choice of weekend activities, I said, "Sure."

After we made our date, I had a panic attack. I recalled the *Honeymooners* episode where Ralph lies to his boss, an avid golfer, about his passion for the game to stand a better chance of getting a promotion that he desperately wants. Of course, the boss invites him to play, and on the eve of their golf date, Ralph is in a frenzy. Neighbor Ed Norton tries to teach ol' Ralphie boy everything he always wanted to know about golf but was afraid to ask in one very long night in the Kramden's kitchen/living/dining room.

I didn't exaggerate, however. Not about my skill. I said that I was an average golfer, who had taken several lessons and needed a few more. I did, however, speak somewhat hyperbolically about my love of the game. I don't know why, exactly. I guess it was the word "love" that I longed to hear come out of my mouth or, in this case, have my fingers type on the keyboard.

My gut told me that I could trust this guy with my address, so when Paul offered to pick me up at my building on Saturday morning at ten, I accepted. Besides, the security in my condo was tight and I never give out my apartment number. He said he'd be driving a 2003 red Toyota. At least we had cars in common, although my Celica was much older. But it *was* burgundy, which I've discovered blends quite well with rust.

I obsessed about what to wear on the date. I actually modeled several LizSport golf outfits for Nancy one evening, who voted hands down for the beige and white ensemble. She said it matched my shoes perfectly. I had almost forgotten about those saddle shoes that all the golfers wear. Fortunately, I had picked up a pair on sale a few years earlier when I was taking lessons. A hat? Absolutely not. That's a guaranteed bad-hair day. But I couldn't have my hair blowing in my face, obstructing my view of the ball. A visor would work, and I had the perfect one . . . cream colored with a white terry-cloth lining. At the very least, I was determined to look the part.

Oh, no. What about my thighs that had started to resemble cottage cheese these last few years? Maybe this was Paul's strategy: let's see how these Internet cuties look in shorts. That bastard. I'll show him. I'll wear pants, although the weather was predicted to be in the mid-eighties—a number I'd never see as my golf score. Maybe I'll just back up to the tee. The legs are passable from the front. It's the backs that are starting to look like road maps.

I obsessed about the date with Paul, much to my own surprise. Perhaps it was because he emailed me a few more times during the week, and I thought that we were starting to connect. I must have wanted this one to work out badly if I was willing to spend half my Saturday playing golf. I needed to tell someone the location of my date, in the event that I never returned. Linda was out of town, so I told Nancy exactly where I'd be, but no one else, as I knew that my other friends would be suspicious of why I chose to be on a golf course on one of the two precious days of my treasured weekend.

On Thursday evening, my phone rang. It was my newly-appointed sports fashion consultant, Nancy, who apparently was quite invested in this big date.

"Hi, Nance," I said. "What's up?"

"Estee Lauder Magnascopic," she replied.

"Hello? Is this a telemarketer?" I asked, somewhat confused.

"Mascara. It's new and it's waterproof. Guaranteed," she said.

"What are you talking about, Nancy? Even if it's on sale, I don't buy mascara because I never wear it. You know that. They all make my eyes itch, even the ones that claim to be hypoallergenic."

"Francine. This is your big chance to play up one of your nicer features. Every man is a sucker for pretty eyes. And even if it's going to be hot out, honest to God, this stuff doesn't run, so it couldn't possibly bother you."

I could see it now: Tammy Faye Bakker teeing off. Or Bette Davis as Baby Jane, skipping down the fairway.

"Thanks for the tip, but I'm not wearing mascara. A flake could get in my eye and ruin my game," I went on.

"Well, at least use an eyebrow pencil. And Clinique has a new matte powder that works wonders in hot weather," Nancy recommended.

I was beginning to get nervous. I had too many things to remember. Not to mention I hadn't picked up a golf club in a year and there was no time to get to a driving range. Oh, well. I was a Girl Scout once. *On my honor, I will do my best.*

Saturday morning rolled around sooner than I expected. Nonetheless, allowing myself three hours to get ready, I was downstairs waiting with clubs slung over my shoulder, a visor on my forehead, and a smile on my face, when a ruby-red Camry pulled up in front of my building. A kind-looking man got out and extended his hand.

"Francine? I'm Paul," he said.

"Hi, Paul. It's good to meet you. Are we all set?"

"Let me have your bag," he answered, as he popped open his trunk and put it into the cleanest storage compartment I'd ever laid eyes on. Except for his set of Pings, which looked like they had been freshly polished, I didn't see one article of clothing, an old paper cup, a pencil, a newspaper, or even a blanket. Nothing. My friends always joked that if I got stranded on the side of the road, I could live for days out of my car. What was that other motto? *Be prepared.*

As we pulled into the parking lot of a lovely public course in the suburbs, it occurred to me that if we were going to carry our bags, I'd be dead by the eighth hole. Fortunately, Paul secured a golf cart, checked us in for our 10:57 tee time (I'll never understand those precise golf hours), and off we went.

Paul was an excellent golfer. One might even say intense. I asked him to tee off first on each hole as I had no idea what this course was like. It was tough. Very tough. When I made a few awful shots, Paul looked appropriately embarrassed for me. But, we seemed to be having a good time. The sun was shining, the temperature was just right, and I had no mascara to worry about dripping down my cheeks. Although I was out of practice, I actually found this fun.

Around the seventh hole, there was a foursome who was gaining on us. I could tell that Paul was getting anxious, so I suggested that they play through. The mere thought of four seasoned golfers staring at me as I teed off made me a wreck. Paul invited them to proceed ahead of us and, thankfully, they took him up on his offer.

We had a soda and he offered me a stick of Juicy Fruit on the ninth hole, and just as I was about to ask Paul about his work, he looked at his watch and said, "Gotta keep going." And with that, we took off in the cart. It was a good thing that I had chosen a visor, as a hat surely would have flown off my head.

By the fourteenth hole, I was getting bone tired . . . the kind of aching exhaustion you feel when you have the flu. I didn't realize how out of condition I had become over the past year. I had been spending most of my free time sitting in front of a computer while others, like Paul, were walking five miles a day, swinging a stick, trying to hit a little white ball and doing a magnificent job of it. He truly was a superb golfer.

By the time I teed off on the sixteenth hole and saw the ball roll only a few dozen feet, I couldn't go on. I walked over, picked up my golf ball, put it in my pocket, and said "I think I'll ride out this hole." In fact, I skipped the next one, too, rallying to play the eighteenth so I wouldn't humiliate Paul in the event he ran into anyone he knew on the final green.

He tallied his score, and I asked him not to even bother with mine. He just smiled. We walked over to his car, he put my clubs back into his pristine trunk, and he drove me home. On the way, we chatted about our kids, our jobs, and our hobbies, but I couldn't get a handle on his interest level in me. I, on the other hand, definitely considered this guy one of my more promising candidates. After all, he could golf and chew gum at the same time.

When we pulled up in front of my building, I had a momentary dilemma. Should I ask him up to my place for a cool drink? Was it too soon? Should I wait for the second date? I didn't want to seem too forward. It turned out that I had nothing to fret about. Paul solved the problem for me. He got out of his car, walked back to the trunk, removed my clubs, handed them to me, and said, "I hope you had fun, Francine. Your short game isn't bad, but you need to work on your drives. A few more lessons should do the trick. Take care." And with that, he smiled, shook my hand, and got back into his car.

I don't know if he watched me walk into my building or if he just drove away. I hope it was the latter, because my clubs and I actually got stuck in the revolving door and the doorman had to come to my rescue. I was far more embarrassed in the lobby of my building than I had ever been on any golf course.

As I rode up in the elevator, I thought about getting ready for this big golf date . . . about my evening with Nancy, helping me choose just the right outfit. I thought about fixing my hair that morning, applying an ever-so-light touch of makeup. I wanted to make a nice impression. I wanted to look good, and I think I did. So why, then, did I feel so bad? No, "bad" wasn't the right word to describe what I was feeling. I was feeling like a prop. Incidental. Passed over. It reminded me of elementary school, when I was never once chosen to be on a sports team. I was a sickly kid for most of those grade school years and my athletic prowess was nil, so I spent much of my time on the sidelines, having just recovered from my latest bout of strep throat, watching my classmates have fun on the field.

As I walked into my apartment, I was fighting back tears. Rejection felt just as bad now as it did back then.

10

Reprieve

THE FOLLOWING MONDAY, I arrived home from work and instead of heading over to the computer to check to see if any little red flags were raised, I called Linda and left a message on her machine, asking her to arrange a time when she, Nancy, and I could get together for dinner. After flying around in cyberspace for the past several months, I needed to make an emergency landing and touch base with my friends. We talked fairly regularly. I called them to chat about the latest episode of *NYPD* . . . they checked in with me a few times a week to see if I was still alive. They undoubtedly wanted neither guilt nor blood on their hands in the event that my last date turned out to be Ted Bundy, Jr. But now I simply wanted to see them in person and reevaluate these last several months.

A few hours later, my phone rang. I checked the caller ID. It was Nancy. I picked it up on the second ring.

"Hi, Francine. What's wrong?" said a frantic voice.

"Hi, Nancy. Nothing's wrong. I'm fine. How are you?"

"No, really. What's going on?" she said. "Linda called me and said that you want to have dinner and that I should arrange it as soon as possible because she was too swamped to set things up. So that's why I'm calling. Is everything okay?"

"Everything's fine. I just miss both of you. I've been so busy with work. And this Internet dating scene is starting to wear me down. I could use some girlfriend time, that's all. You know what I mean? So, when can we get together?" I asked.

"How's Wednesday? We compared calendars and Linda and I are both free that night, so if you are, too, it's a go. Are you?"

"Well, I have my salsa dance class at the health club on Wednesday nights, but I guess I could skip it. Last week, we were short one person, so I did the merengue with the locker room attendant who was out in the hall. The instructor invited her to come in and be my partner because I was the only one without one. You should have seen us. We were quite a pair. Actually, that woman's hips could move," I rambled.

"Francine, sounds like you really need to meet us. We'll see you at Café Louie's at six on Wednesday. I've got to go. Take care. Bye." And with that, she hung up. I was too tired to turn on my computer, television, stereo, or radio. I glanced at my mail for critical correspondence and my closet for the next day's attire, brushed my hair and my teeth, and fell into bed.

That night, I dreamed that my father and I were walking down the street, holding hands. He said that he was going on a trip and that he'd be gone a long time. He went on to say that he had tickets for my mother and brother and that he needed Bob to go, too. It was some kind of important business trip. I asked him where they were going and when he thought they'd be back, because I needed Bob at home. But he didn't answer. We just kept walking, and every once in awhile, he'd stop, turn to me, and give me a tight hug. And when he stepped back, I saw that his face was wet with tears.

I jolted upright in bed and wondered if I had missed hearing the alarm clock and was late for work. The digital numbers read 2:42. It was the middle of the night. My heart was pounding as I got out of bed and shuffled into the kitchen to get a glass of water. I brought it back into the bedroom, took a sip, and started to cry, softly at first. But then the quiet whimpers turned into wretched sobs. I put a pillow over my mouth so that I wouldn't awaken the neighbors. The pain had returned. No, that's not exactly right. It had never gone away.

Linda called me the following afternoon. She said that we were still on for dinner on Wednesday evening, but that instead of meeting at the restaurant, she and Nancy were bringing dinner over to my place. It would be more comfortable, more casual, and we could really "get down and talk." I didn't have to do a thing, she assured me. From wine to dessert, they were taking care of the menu.

"You only have to provide the place," Linda said. "And for God's sake, don't start overhauling it or calling in a cleaning service. We're your best friends. It'll just be more fun to have no men around, which is why *you* have to be the hostess. We'll see you at six. Bye." And with that, she hung up.

No men around. Oh, sure. If anyone needs a safe, manless haven, just hop on over to Francine's. Come on, she didn't mean anything by that remark. Linda and Nancy were married. And their husbands were always underfoot. Well, at least Nancy's was. Linda's was occasionally under *some* female's foot or other body part, but that was another story altogether. It made sense that if the girls wanted their night out to be in, it needed to be over at my place. I was looking forward to Wednesday evening more than I had looked forward to anything in a long time . . . certainly more than I had anticipated any of my dates these past few months, including Paul.

My phone rang at 5:45 on Wednesday night. It was my doorman announcing Linda's and Nancy's arrival. They were early and I was happy that it would take the elevator about five minutes to bring them up to my floor as it gave me that much more time to shove some mail in a drawer and throw a few pairs of shoes in my closet. I admit I was a neat freak. Not obsessive compulsive, but there had been so much illness and chaos in my life that had been out of my control these last five years, that keeping an orderly environment was something finally within my power.

I heard a strong knock at my door just as I was putting a pair of pumps on the shelf, and I flung it open without asking who was there.

"Hi, girlfriend," Linda said.

"You look tired," added Nancy, as they both walked in.

"Thanks a lot. I'm exhausted, but I didn't know it showed. I was up most of the night. Come on in. What have we here? Two shopping bags full of food?" I asked.

"Only one is food. Chinese from Min-Lo's Garden. They have the best pot stickers this side of Shanghai. We brought chopsticks so you won't even have to wash a utensil. The other is our idea bag," continued Linda.

"Our what?" I asked, feeling my stomach tighten.

"Our idea bag," Nancy confirmed. "This is going to be a 'working dinner' for the three of us."

"I thought that we were going to just hang out tonight," I said with a tinge of disappointment in my voice.

"We are, Francine. We're going to eat, drink this," said Linda as she held up a bottle of sake with a design of red dragons on the label, "and help you figure out stuff."

"What stuff? I'm figuring out my life on my own, thank you," I retorted, fighting back tears.

"And doing a stellar job of it," continued Linda.

She must have seen the tears in my eyes, because she immediately placed the shopping bags on my kitchen counter and put her arms around me.

"Francine, forgive me. That remark was 'uncalled for' as my mother would say. We're your friends. We love you. And we want to help you. We want to hear all about your email escapades and then we're going to do some market analysis. Nancy remembered that you're a list maker, so we brought three legal pads, plenty of pens and highlighters, and the latest issue of *Cosmopolitan*. You've been on this cyber search for almost six months now, and we just think that it's time to regroup, reassess, and refocus," Linda said.

This was beginning to sound like graduate school.

"And besides," Nancy continued, "we want to experience

how the single woman hunts . . . vicariously. You have to show us the array of candidates out there in space, so we can eat our little hearts out."

"Let's eat some food, first," I said. "I don't know about the two of you, but I'm feeling faint." I really *was* feeling light-headed and I hadn't had even one sip of sake, although Nancy had already uncorked the bottle and poured each of us a full glass.

Linda set everything on the coffee table, removed a few pillows from the couch, and placed them on the floor so we could sit cross-legged around the table. She was a take-charge individual who had managed to see her friends through a variety of crises, although managing her own lately was an entirely different story. We all knew that her husband had had an affair with his secretary, a woman thirty years his junior . . . a transgression that supposedly was past history with present ramifications. Linda hadn't slept with him since the affair ended a year ago, saying that she needed time to recoup the trust before she could ever give herself up to him again. I wondered why she simply hadn't divorced him, although never having been divorced, I knew that it wasn't fair of me to judge. But if I *was* a judge, my brother used to comment, I would be all black or white. "No gray for Judge Franny," he sarcastically joked. I got his point and knew that he was right. There's always room for error. My tolerance for the forgive-and-forget practice, however, was pretty low, although I knew that I needed to be more broad-minded in this imperfect world. Still, it was Linda's husband who seemed to be the *broad* minded one, as I recently had seen him in the window of O'Toole's, hovered over a candlelit dinner table for two with some leggy redhead who had her hand in his. I had wrestled with what to do or say to Linda about what I had observed, but I decided to keep it to myself, accepting the fact that I was going to be uncomfortable either way. Besides, it's usually the messenger who gets shot.

We ate and drank for what seemed like hours, and then Linda commanded, "Okay, Francine. Lead us to your computer. We're taking you cyber shopping."

We went into my den and I logged on and pulled up my Internet identity. Linda and Nancy started to giggle. "How did you come up with *that* name?" Nancy asked.

"They're from Shakespeare's *Twelfth Night*. I figured that it might attract some literary types. Wast I ever wrongeth. One guy actually thought that I was referring to Popeye's girlfriend 'Olive Oil' instead of 'Olivia Viola.' You girls don't know what's out there," I laughed.

"Okay. Let's hit it," said Linda.

I clicked the MATCHES icon, and a long list of names and pictures instantly appeared on my screen.

"Holy shit! I don't believe this. Where can I sign up?" Linda asked.

"You can't. You're supposed to be single. And they claim there are ways they can check your marital status, although I'm not sure how. There was, however, a recent article in the paper about how reputable this online service is. They won't accept racy pictures, off-color remarks, anything even bordering on lewd," I explained, for once feeling like a woman in the know.

"How boring," Nancy commented. "I was hoping to get together for dinner and a thrill all in the same night."

"Wait, look at that one," Linda exclaimed. "Back it up. You're scrolling down too fast, Francine. Look at those biceps. Come on, let me switch seats with you and I'll read his profile aloud. Just sit back, girls, and close your eyes." She cleared her throat, dramatically. "'I am a renaissance man who loves old Woody Allen movies. Equally at ease in a tux or denim, but prefer the latter. Looking for that special someone to laugh with, cry with, share home-cooked, romantic dinners with in front of the fireplace and take long walks with in the forest preserves. Basically, I'm tired of going it alone and am looking for a significant other to ride the waves with by day and snuggle down with by night. Must be open to new experiences. Little or no baggage, please. Need to make at least as much money as me.'"

Nancy was laughing so hard that some of her sake actually came back up through her nostrils. I, on the other hand, was becoming immune to all of these narratives.

"Let me translate," I said. "What we have here is a guy who lifts weights, lives in his blue jeans, doesn't want to go out for dinner, wants a piece of ass, is probably into kinky sex, and thinks a date is watching *Annie Hall* on video. And I'm really going to go romping in the forest preserves with some total stranger. Oh, yeah, and he's looking for financial security. Not to mention he probably flunked English. It's 'make as much money as I,' not 'me.' Next, please."

"God, you're good," said Nancy.

"And brutal," added Linda. "I think he's kind of cute in that Boss tee shirt."

"Great. Then you respond to him," I answered. "Come on, keep going so you can see firsthand what I've been talking about these past months."

"Okay, here's one who's not so bad. Except for that rug on his head. But you could talk him into au natural after a few dates. Listen up, girls: 'I am a retired military man who is living out my dream. I follow every baseball game with a passion. When the weather gets cold up here, I head out to my place in Arizona where I hang out with the Cubs at spring training. My fantasy dinner guest? Ron Santo. My most prized possession? His autograph. Anyone interested in playing ball?'" Linda continued.

"Now there's my man," I said. "I don't remember when I last sat through nine innings, let alone when I was able to make contact with a sixteen-inch softball. Of course, there's the 'playing ball' double-entendre. See what I mean? Two for two. Care to continue?"

Nancy was now stretched out on the floor, clutching the bottle of sake and chanting in a loud voice, "Yes, yes, keep going, don't stop. More. This is great." Anyone listening outside my door would think I had some wild orgy going on.

"Here's one. He's handsome. Don't look at the tattoos. They can be removed," Linda continued. "Okay, here goes: 'I am an elementary school teacher by day and a writer by night. I've been working on my book for the past two years. It's a combination of historical fiction and biography. I'll be off all summer and would love to have someone read my manuscript, help me with revisions, give me ideas, and just spend time with me. Any good editors out there who would like a preview of the next, great American novel?' Okay, Francine, I know what you're thinking," Linda said.

"That this is one of the most self-centered guys in cyberspace? You're right. Maybe I could put up his bulletin board and prepare his lesson plans for the new school year, too. You forget. I dated a self-absorbed man for too long. Next," I said.

"Who, Barry? I thought the only thing he absorbed was alcohol. Okay. Let's see what else we have here. Whoa. Now there's a big dude. He lists 'a few extra pounds' for 'body type'" Linda remarked.

"Let me see. Oh, him? Keep going. I already spoke to that guy a few weeks ago. Body type was nothing compared with our email exchange. Doesn't anyone pay attention to spell check? As I recall, he was looking for a 'relashunship' to fill those 'lonsum' nights," I said.

"I know a very bright lawyer who can't spell worth a damn. He has his secretary compose all of his correspondence for him," Nancy yelled from the floor, where she was still in a supine state.

"Wonderful. Maybe you can find his number and I could start a tutoring business on the side," I quipped.

"Oh, boy. Here's one with possibilities," announced Linda. He's in a tux . . . very cute. His cropped picture obviously had a lady in it, because his right shoulder is covered with long, blonde hair, but who cares?"

"Probably his ex, whom he divorced a few weeks ago. Some of these guys are on the rebound so prematurely you wouldn't believe it. Okay, what does his profile say?" I asked.

"I am an emotionally and financially secure man with two grown children," Linda read. "A country boy by origin, I now live in Pontiac. I am interested in . . ."

"I'm not," I interrupted. "A country guy who has moved on to the booming metropolis of Pontiac? No thanks. I don't even know why these guys appear on my radar screen. I put 'within twenty miles of Chicago' on my preference list. Yet, these geographically challenged ones keeping popping up. Keep going."

"Wait a minute," said Nancy. "My uncle lives in Pontiac. It's not such a bad town. He's head of some huge correctional facility down there."

"Great. If life got boring, we could camp out so we'd be first in line to see an execution. I want a nearby urbanite. Someone who has some of the same interests as I," I said.

"Okay," said Linda, her finger still scrolling downward. "Here's one who *sounds* good, at least."

"What do you mean by 'at least'?" I asked.

"Well, he hasn't posted a photo of himself," Linda replied.

"Uh-oh!" Nancy said, as she took a swig of sake right from the bottle. "Beware of wolves in sheep's clothing."

Linda and I just looked at each other and shrugged. Nancy was beginning to make no sense at all.

"Listen to his profile. It says he has an advanced degree. He's a professional with grown children. He's been divorced for years. He lives right here in Chicago. Francine, I think you need to contact this one. His name is 'Bernie,'" she added.

"Oh, sure. Degreed, professional, divorced Chicagoan. Those are the basics for starting any relationship. See what I mean, girls? You get very little to go on, really. And yet, you get so desperate that you're willing to respond if they live within the requisite mile radius and seem like they can speak in complete sentences. What's his name? Bernie? Well, I can't contact Bernie tonight, because I'm totally drained, but maybe tomorrow. Besides, I think we better log off and move into the kitchen for some coffee to sober up our friend over here, who looks like she's about to pass out," I said, motioning to Nancy who had begun to sing softly, "Someday he'll come along, the man I love. And he'll be big and strong, the man I love."

"Okay, but I want to come back and do this another time. I don't know when I've had so much fun," Linda said. "This is just a riot. I can see why you'd want to run home every night and log on."

"Right. It's really a great social life," I said with genuine sadness.

I brewed a strong pot of coffee, filled three cups, and carried them into the living room. Linda followed with the bag of fortune cookies that had come with dinner. Nancy was now sitting on the couch, the first time I had seen her in an upright position in the last several hours. Thankfully, they had come in Linda's car. Otherwise I'm afraid that I would have had an overnight guest, whether I wanted one or not. Actually, it wouldn't have been so bad to have someone else under my roof all night. I couldn't remember the last time that had happened.

"Here, have a fortune cookie," Linda said, as she handed Nancy and me our destinies sealed in tiny plastic bags.

I immediately recalled a dinner party that my husband and I had given about twenty-five years earlier. We joined our friends in several of those ethnic gourmet groups that were popular in the seventies, and when it was our turn to host, we chose Chinese fare. We topped off dinner with litchi ice cream and fortune cookies that we had purchased in Chinatown. But what made the evening unforgettable was that Bob and I had removed the mass-produced fortunes from the cookies with a pair of tweezers and stayed up for hours the night before, typing new, original fortunes, cutting them, folding them, and slipping them back into the cookies. Our dinner guests were literally falling off their chairs as they read aloud hilarious messages that held special significance for each of them.

"Francine, you're not listening. Nancy, read your fortune again," said Linda.

"Okay. 'Man and his money are easily parted. Usually by a woman.' How true," Nancy said.

"Alright, let's see what mine says," Linda continued. "'You have wisdom and wealth. Hang on to the latter.' Do I see a monetary pattern here?"

"Okay, Francine. Your turn," Nancy said. "The best is always last."

I ripped open the bag, removed my fortune cookie, broke it,

and popped half of it in my mouth. I pulled the fortune out of the other half and stared at it, then turned it over to the other side. I was silent, as tears started running down my cheeks.

"Oh my God, Francine. What's wrong?" Linda asked. "Are you okay? What is it?"

I couldn't answer and I couldn't stop crying.

"I think she's choking on the cookie," Nancy shouted, as she jumped up and started patting me hard between my shoulder blades.

I shook my head, while the tears kept flowing.

"Stop hitting her. She's not choking. It's the fortune. Let me see that," said Linda, as she took the broken cookie and the fortune from my hand. "Well, this is the first time I've ever seen this in all the years I've been eating Chinese. This must be one of those one in a million mistakes.

"What? What does it say?" Nancy asked.

"Nothing," Linda replied. "There's absolutely nothing written on it at all. It's empty . . . completely blank."

11

Bernie

I TOOK A BREAK FROM cyber browsing for a few days. The evening
with Linda and Nancy had been a painful reminder of how different my life had become. I'd been on my own for the last five
and a half years; yet as time continued to march on, it seemed
as though my life had changed only yesterday. If I had been
widowed when my children were young, I know that it would
have been far worse for all of us, especially for them. But losing
a spouse when I had already "lost" my kids to adulthood was
pretty excruciating for me. Your kids are gone, you think that you
have the rest of your life mapped out with your life's partner. And
then, poof . . . it's like drawing your future on one of those Magic
Slate pads and someone comes along, lifts the filmy cover, and
erases everything.

I still had my children, although they were grown now. I had
my sister. I had my friends. And I had my job. Wasn't that enough,
people would ask or imply? Wasn't I better off than many other
women? Women who had little or no education, stuck in dreadful
marriages because they had no alternatives? Single mothers trying to juggle work, families, relationships, all while trying to keep
the lights and heat on? Wasn't I more fortunate than all of these

others? Sometimes the answer was obvious. Other times, I wasn't so sure.

I was, however, certain of one thing. I wasn't going to give up. After a few days' hiatus, I went back to the drawing board: my computer screen.

Bernie, Bernie. Where was he? Maybe he had gotten married in the last few days and was on his honeymoon instead of online. Men's faces and profiles were whizzing by me, as I was scrolling and trolling. Wait a minute. There he was! "I. M. Bernie." Oh, I get it. I *am* Bernie. I read his profile. Fairly innocuous. Okay, what do I have to lose? I took the plunge and contacted him. Let me tell you about my seventh cyber date, Bernie.

There's something about a man in his fifties dressing like he's in his teens. Don't get me wrong. I'm all in favor of keeping abreast of the latest fashions. I am merely pointing out that one can learn a lot about a person by the way he dresses. I am not talking about expensive clothes. I'm talking about taste. I'm talking about style. I'm talking about fashion statements. I'm talking about common sense.

Bernie and I chatted in cyberspace during the week. He said that he had a law degree but that he never practiced law because he chose not to take the bar exam. My translation: He never passed. Nonetheless, he seemed bright, had a long career in the insurance business, was married once, and had been divorced for six years. What more preliminary information did one need? Maybe I should have dug for more data, but I was definitely becoming weary.

When I agreed to meet Bernie at a new restaurant in Wicker Park for lunch, I figured it would be easy to pick him out of a crowd, even though we had never met. He said that he was 5-feet 6-inches tall. Better for dancing, I told myself. He said he had curly hair. Hopefully, not synthetic. Other than these basics, I knew nothing about his appearance, as Bernie had chosen not to post a photo with his profile. And I, after all, was not so shallow as to have looks be a major criterion. Anyway, how difficult would it be to find each other?

I walked into the restaurant and gazed around the room. I was right on time, but I saw no one who resembled a short, fiftysomething, curly-haired Bernie. So I grabbed a table near the window to have a good view of the neighborhood. This one was a magnet for eclectics. Little old ladies in their tennis shoes toting shopping bags. Mothers proudly pushing their babies in their Prego strollers. Adolescents with multicolored hair and many pierced rings on their faces. And this romantic's favorite: partners strolling hand-in-hand. I still get a thrill to see couples of all ages, shapes, sizes, colors, and genders professing their love for one another in front of the whole world. I got so caught up in the parade of passers-by, that I totally missed a man slowly approaching my table. Oh, my God. Could it be? No, impossible. Yet, coming closer was a slight, middle-aged man with shoulder-length, curly hair who was poured into jeans that were at least two sizes too small. He was wearing white athletic socks that were stuffed into wooden clogs. And his biggest fashion don't of all: a bright blue, satin bicycle racing jacket that had about forty-seven colorful emblems and patches sewn all over it. He looked like he was starring in *Breaking Away for Seniors*. I suddenly felt very overdressed in my corduroys, loafers, turtleneck, and blazer. He probably was as disappointed in my chosen attire as I was appalled at his.

"Bernie?" I stammered.

"Francine," he confirmed.

What could I do but offer my hand to his many bejeweled fingers, which extended from a wrist that had a beaded bracelet dangling from it? Of course, I could have kicked myself for choosing a table that was near the window. What if my sister, who lived only a few miles away, happened to walk into this restaurant on a Saturday afternoon? Alright, highly unlikely. But what if one of my friends was passing by and saw me through the window, one of the many who had no idea that I was an Internet dater? Who would they think I was with? Or, worst of all, what if one of my grown children decided to pop into this popular place for a quick bite . . . my children who, I'm proud to say, never dressed this ridiculously in their lives. Although once when my son was in third grade, he clipped one of his father's black, silk tuxedo bow ties onto his red plaid shirt just seconds before the school photographer snapped his class picture. To this day, I still don't know where he found that tie or what he was thinking. But he was eight years old at the time. Bernie was in his fifties.

Before I even could invite Bernie to sit down, he already was partaking of the rolls in the bread basket. Perhaps his clothes gave him an adolescent's appetite. I will say one thing for him—he had nice molars. In short, Bernie may have been a lousy dresser, but at least his table manners matched his appearance.

When the waiter came over to our table, Bernie was the first to order. A man who knows what he wants, I thought to myself, trying to salvage anything from what I feared would be a painfully long lunch. I ordered a bowl of soup to settle my stomach, which already was starting to turn. Let the conversation begin, I thought. After all, what choice did I have? I had never been to this restaurant before, so I had no idea whether there was a window in the ladies room from which I could escape.

"So, do you have children, Bernie?" I asked. And, by any chance, are those their clothes that you're wearing, I thought to myself.

"Yeah, I have three," he said while dunking hunks of bread into olive oil, which he had obtained a few moments before by snapping his fingers at the waiter while holding up the empty cruet. "Two boys and a girl."

"Do they live with you or with their mother?" I queried, hoping that his answer would be with his ex, so that these kids might have a shot at a normal wardrobe and life.

"Neither. They're in college," Bernie replied, with a mouthful, making it sound more like "They're in cottage."

"Oh, how nice," I said. "Where do they go to college?" Exactly one-half minute had passed since this dialogue had begun.

"My oldest son's a senior at a small college in Maine, the younger one is at Dartmough, and my daughter—the baby—is at a conservatory in Northern California."

I see that they all wanted to stay close by, I sarcastically noted to myself.

"How do they like college life?" I asked, as two teenaged girls walked by our table, gawking at Bernie's outfit. This was going to be one long afternoon.

"They love it. My son who's in Maine is majoring in English and is on the debate team. My younger son, the one at 'Hangover,' New Hampshire, is in pre-med. And my daughter is studying voice with a private teacher. She really got a break roommate-wise. She's sharing an apartment with her older cousin who's a junior at a nearby college. They have a lot in common. Her cousin even got her a part-time job where she works. I'm a firm believer that kids should help support themselves. I'm really proud of her."

I was beginning to admire this father's values. Either that or I was grasping.

"What kind of work do they do?" I asked, expecting to hear a description of one of those typical college jobs, like working at the library or writing for the school rag—hopefully a very detailed, time-consuming description so I could start drinking my hot tea, which the waiter had just placed in front of me .

"They're both waitresses at Hooters. They rake in tons of money," Bernie replied.

Hmmm. Seems like they had at least four things in common, I thought.

Although Bernie did most of the talking and chewing—simultaneoulsy—during the rest of our lunch together, I don't remember much more about that afternoon, like what kind of soup I ordered, if I finished it, what other topics we covered, or what route I took driving home. I was too distracted trying to count the exact number of patches on Bernie's jacket. At one point, I got up to thirty-two, but he kept moving around, waving the waiter over to our table for more bread or water. I don't recall my final tally.

I do remember, however, having a head-to-heart talk with myself in the car, which I have been known to do. This was only my seventh Internet date, I told myself. Maybe there were, in fact, eight Wonders of the World. Anyway, I couldn't judge the quality of the whole pageant on the talents of a few of the earlier contestants any more than I could critique an entire meal after sampling several unsavory hors d'oeuvres. (I just wasn't so sure that I had the stomach to make it all the way to dessert). And although I wanted to scream out as if he could hear me, "Yes, Dad, sometimes you *can* judge a book by its cover," I knew that I couldn't let the first few stops ruin the rest of the trip. If nothing else, I was learning a lot about myself. I'm chronically hopeful. I'm surprisingly resilient. I'm an incurable optimist. I'm also a good traveler—and this voyage was still in its maiden stage.

12

Allan

Up until now, I haven't shared many of the cyber headlines floating out there—those captivating captions that we Internet daters were instructed to create. They usually were eye-catching. They sometimes were clever. And they often were revealing. There were a few that I immediately deleted: "Lover Boy," "Jim Shoe," "Gun in My Pocket," "Warm in the Kitchen . . . Hot in the Bedroom," "King of My Castle," and my personal favorite: "Want a Wife Right Now." I pictured this last one's clothes spinning in the dryer and he needed someone to fold. I preferred cryptic captions—combinations of numbers or letters. At least they left something to the imagination. Or down-to-earth subtitles that exposed someone's naïveté.

Allan's moniker was "Tru-gent." His headline was "Classy Act Looking for Same." Not wildly imaginative, but not offensive, either. His photo showed him wearing a suit and tie with his hands folded in his lap. He did look like a true gentleman.

His profile said he that was fifty-eight years old. I liked men who were older than I. My father was eleven years older than my mother, and theirs was a romance straight out of a 1950s movie . . . Audrey Hepburn and Gregory Peck in *Roman Holiday*. My brother was ten years older than I and, growing up, I always preferred his friends to mine. They were savvy. They were sophisticated. They were wise. Besides, age is in one's head.

Enter Allan. The fifty-eight-year-old true gent. The classy act who had many interests that coincided with mine. He liked music, especially jazz. He lived in the heart of the city. He worked out. He was a widower. This was looking good.

Allan was a semi-retired marketing director who knew how to market himself. His well-written email said that he was fascinated by my profile, in particular, my list of guests that I would include at my "fantasy dinner party." Compiling this list was a suggestion of the Internet Dating Gods, who swear that it's a clever way to pique a candidate's interest. When composing mine, I tried to choose well-known people who would speak to my hobbies and interests. There was Plato, reflecting my heritage. Alfred Lord Tennyson, Tom Wolfe, and Studs Terkel were on my list because I enjoy and admire their works. B. B. King would be invited because I've seen him and Lucille bring down the house on several occasions. Luciano Pavarotti would receive an invitation because he sang arias almost as beautifully as my father. Bette Davis would be invited because I've seen every one of her movies and, perhaps, we could recite her lines together. And Woody Allen was included because he always makes me laugh—on a cerebral level, take note, Jack.

Back to Allan. I don't know. Perhaps I'm dyslexic, but Allan was either fifty-eight or eighty-five. You be the judge.

Allan emailed me both his office and his cell numbers, following an Internet dating precaution, no doubt, of never giving out one's number at home. He worked only a few hours a day, so he wanted me to have a way to contact him. His email said that I would have the best chance of reaching him on his cell if I called before five-thirty. I thought he meant in the evening. Allan meant five-thirty in the morning. Allan didn't know me well enough to know that by five-thirty, I've only been asleep for about five and a half hours. So, I tried him at his work number at nine in the morning.

He answered, but said that he'd have to get right back to me, as he was in a meeting. My life is laden with meetings, so I understood perfectly. When he returned my call, we chatted for a few minutes. His voice was a little shaky, but I chalked it up to the first-phone-call jitters. He said that he'd like to meet for a cup of coffee. I suggested a cup of coffee at around seven. After planning where we would meet, he said that he'd double-check to see if the restaurant was open that early. It was then that I realized that he was talking seven A.M. I told him that I was referring to a cup of coffee *after* work, as I usually leave for work at seven-thirty or eight and don't return until about six in the evening. He said that he couldn't drink caffeine that late in the day, or he'd be up all night. I told him that I *never* drank caffeine at any hour, or I'd be up for the rest of my life. I was just using "a cup of coffee" as an expression. He could have decaf. He could have herbal tea. He could have juice. We could choose a place with a liquor license and he could have a glass of wine.

"Not on a school night, Francine. Seven's a little late," Allan advised me.

I was confused. Was this guy a teacher? I thought he was a semi-retired marketing director. Oh, I get it. "A school night" was just an expression, like "a cup of coffee."

"Well, okay Allan. I could meet you on Saturday morning for coffee or tea, if you'd like," I compliantly suggested. I despised this guy already, as I like to sleep in on Saturdays.

"Great, Francine. How about eight?"

"Eight o'clock on a Saturday is a little early for me, Allan. Nine would be better." I was finding my voice again, and it felt good.

"Okay. I guess I could skip my work-out routine one time. I do aqua-aerobics on Saturday mornings from nine-thirty to ten-thirty."

"No, I wouldn't want you to do that, Allan," I said. "Let's meet at eleven. That way, you can make your class and have plenty of time to dry off, too."

"Okey dokey," he said. Where should we meet?"

"You pick it, Allan," I said, hoping that he couldn't detect the edge in my voice. It had taken us over ten minutes to decide on a time. I figured it would be another fifteen to find a location.

"How about Helen's Kitchen on Clark Street?" he said.

"Fine. I'll see you at Helen's Kitchen at eleven o'clock on Saturday morning. Bye." And with that I hung up.

Saturday morning came quickly. I showered, threw on my weekend togs and drove over to Helen's Kitchen. I knew what Allan looked like, so I figured that it wouldn't take me long to find him. I was right. He was standing in line, waiting to be seated.

"Francine?" he said.

"Allan," I answered.

Our waitress, who was wearing a hairnet and a button that said "Hi, I'm Bernice," led us to a booth near the back of the restaurant. We no sooner sat down, than Allan called the waitress back over to our table and asked if we could switch to another booth, as he could feel a draft. For just a brief moment, I thought that Bernice was going to slap him. But instead, she whisked the menus off of the table and took us to another one.

"How's this one?" Bernice asked.

"This one's fine," I answered.

When the busboy brought us our waters, Allan asked if he could have his with no ice. The busboy obviously understood very little English, nodded his head and said, "yes, nice," so I took my spoon and scooped the ice cubes out of Allan's glass and plopped them into mine. I was beginning to resent spending my Saturday morning at Helen's Kitchen when I could have gotten a few more precious hours of sleep. Nonetheless, I'm a trouper. I'm flexible. I can cope. When Bernice came back to take our order, Allan asked her if she had any bran cereal.

"Sure, hon, we have raisin bran."

"Are they currants in the cereal or raisins?"

"Well, the last time I asked—which was never—they were raisins. Isn't that why they call it raisin bran? Besides, I don't even know what currants are," said Bernice.

"Well, okay. I'll have the raisin bran. With soy milk please. I'm lactose intolerant."

"With what?"

"Soy milk," Allan said, his voice getting shakier.

"I'll see what I can do. And for you, sweetie?" she asked, looking at me as she rolled her eyes.

"I'll have an English muffin, toasted, and a cup of decaf," I replied.

"Gotcha."

"So tell me about your job, Allan," I said.

"Well, I'm a marketing consultant. I work about four hours a day. My routine is this: I get up every morning at four forty-five and, after having some hot water with lemon, I do some calisthenics for thirty minutes. Then, after I shower, I read the entire paper while I have breakfast. Usually bran flakes and some fruit. Whatever's in season, although I prefer strawberries and blueberries as they are the best antioxidants of all the fruits. Never melons—they make me bloated. Then, I bicycle to my office at eight. It takes me seven minutes from door to door. After that, I have a meeting or two with my clients, and then at 10:30 I shut my office door, stretch out on the floor and take a fifteen-minute cat nap. You'd be surprised at what those fifteen minutes can do for your stamina. I'm so refreshed, that I can go until noon. Then I have a little lunch—usually something I've packed myself. Cottage cheese, a hard-boiled egg—I scoop out most of the yolk, though, as that's where all of the cholesterol is—some more fruit, and a slice of cheese. Usually mozzarella, as it has the lowest fat content of all the cheeses. Unless you specifically get low-fat cheese, which I don't recommend, as it's very high in sodium. It's kind of a trade-off. High fat or high sodium. I don't know which is worse for me, so I try to watch both."

My head felt like it was in an echo chamber. I could see Allan's lips continuing to move, but I couldn't hear anything coming out of his mouth. He went on and on and on, even after Bernice brought us our food, my decaf and a glass of Allan's soy milk. Every so often I caught a few words like "HDL cholesterol" and "atherosclerosis" and "esophageal reflux."

During the rest of our breakfast, my mind started to wander.

I looked at Allan, who was still talking and eating his cereal. It was obvious that Allan took excellent care of himself. He exercised on a regular basis and, speaking of regular, he had his daily bran flakes. He was into healthy eating . . . fruit, protein, not too much sodium or fat. He napped every day, something I hadn't done since I was three. He went to bed at nine, something I hadn't done since I was seven. He got at least eight hours sleep per night, something I hadn't done since I was twelve.

I admired Allan's discipline. I envied his excellent health. I was in awe of his diligence. I made up my mind right then and there that I would make appointments to get some of those tests that I had been putting off. A stress test. A cholesterol screening. That dreaded colonoscopy. And while power-walking was great, I needed to get into a challenging cardiovascular exercise program. And let's cut out refined sugar. Who needs it, anyway?

I had Allan to thank for these spontaneous resolutions. After all, what I had suspected from our earlier conversation, I now was convinced of: Allan was a wonder. He wasn't fifty-eight and I wasn't dyslexic. I'd bet anything that Allan was a very well-preserved octogenarian.

I split the bill for breakfast and shook hands with Allan, wishing him well on his Internet search. This Tru-gent surely sensed as clearly as I that we were not a match. As I was driving home, I started to reflect on these past cyber dates. Cruising on this Internet journey was enlightening. For one thing, I learned that people are different and that I needed to embark on every date with an open mind. These encounters mimicked life and, as such, I had to be flexible. I needed to adjust my expectations. Not that I was ready to lower the bar so much that I would waste my time with dates that I would never reach compatibility—or anything else— with. But I needed to be realistic. Also, I was learning the valuable lesson that while memories—both good and bad—were powerfully seductive, I needed to leave them behind. These rendezvous were for two, not for three.

Nonetheless, when I arrived home, I immediately headed for my bookcase. I needed a chair to reach the top shelf where the photo albums and scrapbooks were stacked . . . the reminders of my past that I was trying to hide from my everyday present. I paged through them, looking at pictures of Bob's and my first apartment, our first baby, our first house, our first vacation. I thought that these memories would keep growing right into our first retirement home. I closed the albums and put them back up on the shelf, out of view.

While Allan wasn't the man for me, I was beginning to accept the fact that there might never be another guy out there like Bob. Perhaps a reasonable facsimile. But certainly not a carbon copy.

On the one hand, that sobering fact frightened me. On the other hand, the limitless possibilities were beginning to fascinate me.

13

Home

Thinking of Internet dating as an adventure made me recall some of the travels in my life. I felt fortunate to have been born into a family who had relatives living in another country. Long before I had ever met my cousins, we wrote long letters to each other although, even with my trusty English/Greek dictionary, I usually had to have theirs translated by my parents. Looking back, I wondered who translated mine to them, my attempt at using the Greek alphabet being rudimentary, at best, and their knowledge of English being the same. Nonetheless, I had a drawer full of letters from relatives I had never met. We exchanged cards, pictures, and trinkets. I saved the flimsy airmail envelopes with the foreign postmarks and exotic-looking stamps, usually depicting some elegant, stately king. Just knowing that these cousins were a part of me and I of them, living on the other side of the world, gave me a thrill.

When I was twelve, my mother and I took our first trip across the ocean on a ship bound for Greece. The first few days were rough, and I remember spending those days in our cabin, sipping hot tea and eating tiny morsels of dry toast. Then, after a short reprieve, the Adriatic and the Mediterranean met, started dancing, and all hell broke loose. I didn't know which was worse, the sounds of the crashing waves or my wobbly legs and dizziness every time I tried to walk a few feet. My mother had her own worries. I was a skinny kid to begin with and she wrung her hands over my becoming even scrawnier before her eyes. Once the ocean liner completely settled into the Aegean, it was like the end of a war. The blue skies melted into the even bluer sea, and to make up for my lack of caloric intake, my mother indulged my every culinary whim, which meant that my primary diet for the rest of the trip was dessert.

I'll never forget the day that the ship pulled into the port of Piraeus, outside of Athens. The passengers had rushed to the railing, so weary were we of seeing nothing but sea and sky for eleven days. My mother began waving excitedly to the throngs of people on shore, so I did, too. It didn't matter that they were strangers. What mattered was that we had arrived at our destination and new adventures awaited us.

One man who resembled my father was hollering and flapping the air with a handkerchief in one hand while holding a bunch of flowers in the other. He started blowing kisses and he kept hugging the woman next to him, as he pointed toward the ship. I thought he was funny, even comical, and I wondered what his story was. But as the ship's lines were tied to the dock and we came closer to shore, I could see that he was looking right at my mother and me. I could also see that he was using the handkerchief to wipe the tears from his eyes and the perspiration from his forehead.

"That has to be your Uncle Paul," my mother told me. "He's your father's brother. I recognize him from his pictures," she went on to explain. "And that must be your Aunt Tasia. They're here to meet us. They're so disappointed that your father couldn't make the trip with us."

I knew how much my father wanted to accompany my mother and me to his native land to personally introduce us to his family for the first time. He hadn't been back to his home since his mother's funeral about ten years earlier, and he and my mother had talked about his going, the best way to get there, and the most economical. But he didn't get the kind of vacations that made an eleven-day cruise across the ocean an easy and practical mode of travel, and flying was even more expensive in those days, not to mention my mother was petrified to step foot on an airplane. And so, he made all the arrangements for my mother and me to take a train to New York, then to sail from New York to Greece, and finally, for his family to be waiting for us when we arrived.

The ship's gangplank was lowered, and while we began disembarking, my Uncle Paul and Aunt Tasia came rushing toward the long line of passengers, yelling "Yassou, Fotini. Yassou, Efrocini. Welcome to Greece," although the way they said it, it sounded like "We come to Greece." One of the liner's crew had to restrain my uncle, admonishing him from going any further and motioning him to stand back to allow the passengers through. When I studied his face as my mother and I were inching along in line, he looked like a child who could barely wait for his turn to ride on the Ferris wheel, and I felt more like the parent, reserved and patient.

When we finally were free from the line, my Uncle Paul swooped down and picked me up off the ground, twirling me around and around. Tears were streaming down his face. I looked at my mother, whose own face was being smothered with kisses by my Aunt Tasia. They were talking in Greek, and although I had resisted taking Greek lessons as a child, I could understand words like "welcome" and "our home" and "so happy" and "I love you." Then, we exchanged partners, and now it was my aunt who was calling me "her little bird" in Greek and my uncle who was kissing my mother's cheeks, while he kept wiping his eyes. He handed her a bunch of flowers that looked like they had been through a rough day, and my mother's face beamed as if he had presented her with a bouquet of gilded roses. In all of my life, I never had a welcome like the one that I experienced that day and I was convinced that there'd never be a greeting as glorious and memorable for anyone.

After more hugs, kisses, and tears, my uncle and aunt took

our luggage and we all piled into a taxi that sped us to a tiny hotel just outside of Piraeus near Athens. We had a light meal of salad, cheese, olives, and bread in the hotel's outdoor courtyard, and then we checked into two rooms for the night in anticipation of the next day's long journey to my father's tiny mountain village to meet all of his family and the many cousins to whom I had been writing since I was a young child. I asked my mother why we all were staying in a hotel . . . why we weren't staying in my aunt's and uncle's house.

"They don't live in the city, Francine," she explained. "Only wealthy people can afford to have another place in Athens. Their home is in your father's village, over six hours away. That's where they live year-round. Your father made all of the arrangements for the four of us to stay here tonight, and then we'll make the trip to the village tomorrow. Now let's get ready for bed and try to get some sleep," she said, as she turned down the covers on the big bed that she and I would share. I remember being so tired that my arms and legs ached, but I was unable to sleep for more than an hour or two. I hadn't felt this excited since I was five years old on Christmas Eve.

The next morning at seven, there was a knock on the door. My mother had just gotten out of the shower, and I was still in bed. It was my aunt and uncle, all dressed up, she in a flowered dress that wrapped around and tied in front, he in a shiny suit with a shirt that pinched at the neck and a tie that I recognized as my father's.

"Good morning. We wait for you for eat, yes? Then we make trip home," Uncle Paul said, in broken English, his eyes warm and twinkling. My mother assured him that we'd join him downstairs right away.

Within fifteen minutes, we zipped up our bags that we barely had touched the night before, and rode down in the elevator to meet them in the lobby. We had a breakfast of hard-boiled eggs, fruit, yogurt, honey, and toast, and then my uncle directed us to a cab that was waiting in front of the hotel, which we took back to the port where we boarded a ferryboat to the city of Patras. My mother hadn't exaggerated. It was five hours to Patras and then another thirty minutes on a smaller boat to the town of Nafpaktos. From there, we caught a bus to the town of Paralia and then what I thought was the end of the adventure was just the beginning. My father's village and my aunt's and uncle's home were nestled in the mountains at about 1,200 feet elevation. There were no paved roads for cars, only dirt trails for donkeys, our mode of transportation. My uncle rounded up five donkeys in all, one for each of us and one to transport the luggage. I remember my mother making the sign of the cross over and over again while we ascended, watching the small seaside town get even tinier, until it finally looked like one of those foreign postage stamps on the many letters I had saved. As we rode up the mountain, we occasionally passed villagers herding goats, and my uncle would stop the donkey parade to introduce us. "These are Demetri's family, wife and daughter from America," he'd say. "Demetri. America," they'd repeat, and break into a grin.

After an hour's ride, the caravan slowed. My uncle pointed to a tiny church and began speaking in Greek. Tears welled up in his eyes and his voice cracked. My mother translated. The church, which was the epicenter of the village, had been destroyed in an earthquake and my father had sent money to his family monthly so that it could be rebuilt. The villagers renamed the church St. Demetrious, after my father.

A few minutes later, we finally arrived at my father's house, the home where he was born and raised. At least twenty relatives were waiting for us outside. Aunts and uncles and cousins of all ages rushed to my mother and to me, kissing us even before we had a chance to get down from the donkeys, brushing my hair out of my eyes, saying "matia, matia," which my mother explained meant "eyes," they commenting on how I had the same blue eyes—a rarity in the family—as my father's mother . . . my grandmother, a woman whom I had never met but one who, apparently, was very much alive in me.

I'll always remember that first day and night in the village. My cousins took turns taking me into their modest homes, pointing to pictures of me and my family that were proudly displayed on walls, shelves, and tiny tables. At first I thought that they had just put them out, like my mother did when she'd haul out a hideous vase that her aunt had given to my parents for their wedding anniversary whenever she came to visit. But it didn't take long to realize that their welcoming love was genuine, as later that day we visited many other homes in the village unannounced, homes that had similar photos of my father, my mother, my siblings and me hanging on their walls. I soon came to understand that my father was a hero in their eyes. He was forced to leave home at thirteen—just about the same age that I was then—to go to America to make a living to help support his family and his village. I had heard numerous stories of how the medicine he regularly sent to his sister had kept her alive through a serious illness. How he had brought two of my older cousins to the states and had put them through college. How the packages of dried goods he loaded in cartons and shipped back home had sustained the villagers through terrible droughts that neither olives nor vegetables could survive. And now I saw with my own eyes how the clothes that I had outgrown and had helped my parents pack in boxes were being proudly worn by my younger cousins.

We had a fine feast in the church square that evening, and my cousins tried to teach me to play soccer. We ran around and laughed and it didn't matter that we didn't speak each other's language. We were cousins. We were part of one another.

When it became dark, we went into my father's home, into the same room that he and his brothers and sisters had shared more than fifty years earlier. Since there was no electricity in the village, there was no option but to turn in for the night. A few candles were lit so that we could wash our faces and hands before getting into the bed that my mother and I shared. As I kissed my aunt and uncle goodnight, I thought about the day that had started out in the port town of Piraeus, how we had traveled by cab, ferry, kayak, bus, and donkey to the best welcome I would ever receive . . . to the most memorable one I thought I would ever experience.

At about three in the morning, there was a loud knock on the door. My uncle's voice was the first one I heard and then my aunt's and, soon after that, my mother's. Something was wrong. What was the commotion? Who was this intruder calling in the middle of the night? My uncle lit a candle and headed toward the door. The house was so dark that I remember how fascinated I was that he could even walk without bumping into things. I stayed close behind my mother, clutching her nightgown, as she followed my aunt who was right behind my uncle. He swung the door open. At first I thought it was a ghost, an apparition. But as my uncle held the candle beneath the visitor's face, I saw that it was no vision. It was my father himself.

My uncle's shoulders began to shake, followed by his whole body. He was trembling and it frightened me. But my mother put her hand on my shoulder, the same hand that had told me many times before that everything was alright.

My father and his brother, Paul, had not seen each other in ten years. Now, with candle wax dripping onto the floor, my uncle threw his arms around him, crying "Demetri, Demetri." They stood and looked at each other, and then hugged and kissed some more. My mother ran over to my father and took his face in her hands, as if she needed proof that he was really standing in the doorway. She asked him how he had traveled, and he explained that while he didn't have the time to sail to Greece, he managed to make last-minute arrangements to take a week off from work and to fly to Athens. He said that he didn't care about the cost . . . that finally seeing his two families together for the first time, even if just for a week, was better than never seeing them together at all.

"But how did you know how to get here all by yourself, especially at night," I asked my father, having just experienced the complex and arduous journey the previous day.

He simply answered, "You never forget your way home, Francine."

My Uncle Paul took my father's small duffel bag, set it down on the kitchen floor, and then, almost in unison, they both turned and walked out of the house into the night, their arms around each other. I could see the flicker of the candle that my uncle still held as my mother and I watched them from the door.

"Why don't you go with them?" I asked my mother.

"No, no," she said, wiping her eyes with the sleeve of her nightgown.

"Why not? Where are they going?" I persisted.

"They're just going for a walk. Your father is home, now."

I knew that I would never witness a grander reunion than the one that I had seen that night between my father and my Uncle Paul. And that was when I began to realize something else, too, something that would stay with me forever: adventure was everywhere . . . on a ship sailing across the sea, in a tiny mountain village, all around me, even back home.

14

Craig

I WASN'T FAMILIAR WITH THE acronym MITN, until my friend Amy explained it to me a few years ago. We were sitting in a coffee shop one day, and she was talking about her parents. She said that her mother had been complaining to her that her father's and her sex life had really deteriorated over the last decade.

"I mean, talk about MITN," Amy said to me, as her face blushed.

I could have appeared savvy, and just nodded. But I had no idea what she was talking about, so I simply said, "What's MITN?"

"You know: more information than necessary. I mean, these are my parents, for God's sake. I don't even want to imagine my parents doing it at *all*, let alone listen to details of how things have gone south for them in bed."

Now, years later, I could relate. My ninth date, Craig, definitely was an MITN guy. Craig's emails were very well-written, which is what attracted me to his profile. No, he didn't post a photo of himself, but I was beginning to feel superficial when I'd see a candidate's picture and immediately hit the DELETE button. The guy seemed intelligent and suggested that we meet after work one night, so I thought, "Why not?" My screening stamina was definitely beginning to wane.

Craig said in his emails that he had two residences, a house in the suburbs and a cabin in Michigan. He went up to the cabin every other weekend, sometimes driving straight up the peninsula, which was an eleven-hour trip. Other times, he'd camp out overnight on the way to the cabin. He definitely was the outdoorsy type, which had me a little concerned, as my idea of roughing it is a Red Roof Inn with no cable. Nonetheless, we were meeting for a drink at a local bar, not a weenie roast 'round a campfire. So, we made a date. He told me that I'd have no trouble recognizing him. "Many of the ladies tell me that I look like an aging Clark Gable," he wrote.

I arrived at the place feeling like Scarlett O'Hara, as I looked around. There were only two men at the bar. One was a dead ringer for Buddy Ebsen from his *Beverly Hillbillies* days and the other guy looked like he was in his fifties. Please don't let it be Grandpa Clampett, I prayed. As I got closer, I could see that the fifty-ish one was sporting a mustache, which is where the Craig/Clark similarity ended. Maybe he meant the alliteration. No, I was getting confused. That was Frank.

"Craig?" I asked.

"Francine," he replied. "Excuse me for starting without you," he said as he held up his tumbler. "What are you drinking?"

"I'll have a Pinot Grigio," I said. Have to vary those whites, I thought to myself.

"One Pinot Greegiack for the lady," he said to the bartender, who suppressed a smile. "Well, it's good to meet you, Francine. I don't know how long you've been alone or when you got started on this Internet dating thing, but for me it's been too damn long."

"I've been an ID—Internet Dater—for about four months now," I said, feeling proud of my newly created acronym, which was probably old to everyone else.

"Well, I've been doing this for about a year, and it's high time I met a pretty little lady like yourself," he went on. "My last wife was mighty attractive, but we just couldn't get along. Fought like cats and dogs all the time. Except in the bedroom. We never had any trouble in that room of the house. She was a hot little number. In fact, last July—six months after the divorce—she came over to get the rest of her clothes out of the bedroom closet and, well, one thing led to another and before we knew it, we were naked as two jaybirds, shaking the sheets."

I wasn't prepared for this revelation, especially in the first sixty seconds of our conversation, and some of my wine must have gone down my windpipe, because I started to cough and couldn't stop.

"Are you alright, hon?"

"Yes, I'll be okay. I just need to run to the ladies room," I said, as I got up and walked to the back of the bar, coughing all the way.

When I returned, Craig said, "For a minute, I didn't think that you were gonna come back. Figured you'd escaped."

If only.

"So, where was I? Oh, yeah. My second wife. Anyway, we had some fun that afternoon, but afterwards the same old fighting started again. I knew then and there that the divorce was inevitable."

I wanted to get off of the second wife, even if Craig didn't, literally.

"Do you have children?" I asked. It's always wise to review the candidate's email right before heading out on an Internet date, but I had completely forgotten and now my mind was crammed with a plethora of profiles.

"I have three: one daughter from my first marriage and two sons from my second. It took my first wife five and a half years to get pregnant. We tried everything. Specialists. Medication. Injections. Nothing worked, even though we spent half of our life in bed. My motto was 'If at first you don't succeed, try, try again.' Now fertility wasn't a problem with the second missus. I looked at her on our second date—okay, I did a little more than look—and bingo, nine months later, my first son was born. No, we never did have any trouble in that department," he repeated.

A wave of nausea was blanketing me. Maybe from all of the pregnant talk.

"So where are your kids now?" I asked, trying to keep us on another more comfortable topic, although Craig looked mighty comfy to me, as he moved his bar stool right up against mine.

"Well, my daughter teaches school in Phoenix. She's the only one who has made me a granddad, although she never married the bastard, thank God. But she's quite a mother and I mean that word in the best sense. My oldest son is a computer programmer in Milwaukee. He's not married, but he's going with this great gal. What a body on that one. She's a lingerie model for catalogues and magazines and stuff like that. And my youngest son is still at home with his mother. He'll be there for awhile. He's bipolar. We don't know when all of that started. One day he's as happy as a lark and the next day he can't get out of bed. He's on four different kinds of medication, which is costing us a fortune."

"Oh, I'm really sorry," I said. "But they're doing all kinds of research on mental illness. So you shouldn't give up hope."

"Who said anything about mental illness? He's a happy kid— at least *half* of the time. That's more than I can say about most people. Take my boss, for instance. Now there's a nutcase. Yesterday, we had our weekly staff meeting and he's freaking out because there were fingerprints on the conference room table. He actually took out a can of Lemon Pledge and started spraying. That's what I call mental illness."

"More like a disorder . . . obsessive compulsive," I said.

"Whatever. You a psychologist?"

"No, but I read a lot. Anyway, I'm sure that your son will be fine."

"Damn right he'll be fine. If my ex doesn't totally screw him up. Figuratively speaking, of course. One of the many things we fought about was how to raise our kids. She was real lenient. No curfews for those boys. If they wanted to stay out until two or three in the morning, she said, 'No problem. Just let us know where you'll be.' If they wanted to drink beer in high school, she'd have one with them. If they wanted to smoke a joint, she showed them how to roll one. She said she'd rather they did it in the house. Needless to say, she was the popular parent."

"Oh, that's awful."

"What's awful? My kids?"

"No. The way your ex let them do anything they wanted," I said nervously. I was beginning to feel uneasy.

"Listen, I didn't say she was a bad parent. I mean, would I let my son live with her now if I thought she was a bad parent? Did I use the word 'bad?' I don't remember saying that. I think I used the word 'lenient.' 'Lenient' is not synonymous with 'bad.' Do you think it is? Is that what you're thinking?"

I was thinking that Craig was probably due for his next dose of Lithium.

"No, not at all. Lenient is not bad. Actually, lenient can be very good. Listen, Craig. Unlike your boys, I *do* have a curfew. I have an early morning meeting. But it was a real pleasure meeting you," I said as I stood up and extended my hand, feeling the tension shoot from my fingertips to my shoulder.

"Hey, is this the brush-off? I think I know the brush-off when I see it. Okay, I get it. You don't have to hit me over the head. That's what I always used to tell my wives. You don't have to hit this guy over the head. Good-bye, Francine. I hope you find what you're looking for."

Right now, I was considering looking for a cop to escort me outside. I hurriedly left the bar, ran to my car, which was parked a half block away, jumped in and locked the door. Find what I was looking for? Maybe someday, I thought to myself. But for now, I was beginning to understand what I *wasn't* looking for, as I put the key in the ignition and drove off, still trembling. I was thankful that I had followed the ID rules and told Linda what bar I'd be meeting Mr. Gable in, just in case. And I was grateful to Craig for sharing MITN. It resulted in an F & L date with him . . . first and last.

I decided to take the long route home to quell my nerves. That wasn't the only reason. I also had an ache to drive down memory lane. The apartment building where my parents brought me home as a newborn, the next one where I spent the years from kindergarten until college, and the first one that Bob and I moved into as newlyweds were all within a mile radius of one another on the north side of Chicago. And except for a short lapse to the suburbs, we returned to the city that was in our blood. To the lakefront, where families still gathered to barbecue and play softball; the small, quaint parks that dotted the Gold Coast; the expansive museums that made even the most sophisticated eyes widen; the ethnic corridors; the notorious el; the Loop; even the depleted neighborhoods that were years away, if ever, from a Starbucks all held a fascination for us. It was called the "city that works," and it worked for me.

As I drove down my street, I could almost see my father, feebly trying to play catch with me on a Sunday afternoon. He didn't know a thing about sports or games, having given up his youth at thirteen when he—the oldest of eight children—was sent alone to America to earn a living for his impoverished family back in the old country. When he would shame us into finishing our dinner by telling us that there were children starving in Europe, he knew them by name. He worked twelve-hour days for sixty-six of his seventy-nine years, leaving little time for throwing balls around or for any other forms of recreation.

I could almost hear my mother, calling out to me from one of the windows of our third floor walk-up. I could see her tossing me her change purse with a short grocery list and some dollars tucked in it. I felt so important, as she trusted me to fetch a few foodstuffs that she would transform into a sumptuous meal. I also felt embarrassed when she would make me walk all the way back to our friendly, neighborhood grocer's if I was overcharged or, worse yet, undercharged.

I could almost make out my sister and brother sitting in the front seat of our father's 1955 two-toned blue sedan, the keys in the ignition, listening to the radio and smoking cigarettes. That car was one of their private, little-sisters-not-allowed hangouts, and I could still feel the mixture of hurt and jealousy.

As I turned the corner to head back home, the Righteous Brothers had just begun singing "Unchained Melody" on the radio. It was Bob's favorite. We could be at a crowded party in Madison or at a formal dinner dance twenty years later and, when I heard that song, I knew that no matter where Bob was in the room, he'd find me, excuse me from small talk with the other guests, and whisk me out on the dance floor. We loved to dance, sometimes in our bathrobes as we were getting ready for work in the morning, other times at night in our bedroom, with the door locked, the lights dimmed and the music playing loudly to drown out the passion.

The song also made me think of 1997. I was the first sibling to marry and the first to bury. The day that my sister drove with me to the funeral home so that I could make arrangements for Bob's service, I turned on the radio and that same song came on. She said, "Isn't this the song they played in that movie, *Ghost*?" I pulled the car over to the curb and began to cry. She tried to console me, assuring me that she'd stay with me all day and all night . . . anything it would take to get me through the funeral. She didn't know and I couldn't begin to tell her. That was "our song." He was gone. And I would never dance with him again.

As I drove back to my apartment building, I noticed how alive the streets were. I passed movie theatres, quaint cafés, neighborhood joints, and glitzy hotels with doormen and their ever-ready smiles. I thought of songs that I grew up with when I was a kid. My father crooning to my mother, "Ah, Sweet Mystery of Life" and singing to me, "The Way You Look Tonight." Lullabies, as I rocked my own babies to sleep. Years later, as their guitars rocked and robbed us of ours. What I wouldn't give now for one of those musical, sleepless nights.

Yet I *knew* that there were more melodies waiting to be played. Different tunes, distinct tempos, complex notes, and unfamiliar rhythms, perhaps. But captivating music, just the same.

15

Jeff

I ARRIVED HOME FROM MY date with Craig and tossed my mail onto the ever-growing stack on my kitchen counter. I played my phone messages. There was one from Linda and one from my sister. Linda knew that I had an Internet interlude and was checking in. My sister knew nothing of the sort, or she'd be checking *me* in. I felt a tad deceitful not sharing my secret life with my sis but, then again, it was bad enough that my public life was often under her scrutiny. Maybe someday, but not now. I'll call her tomorrow. On the other hand, I had to return Linda's call tonight or I feared she might place one to the Bureau of Missing Persons. Actually, it made me feel safe to know that someone, in addition to me, was aware of my cyber schedule . . . another security measure taken by us Internet daters.

I was relieved to get her answering machine. "Hi, Linda. It's Franny. I'm home, unharmed. Well, at least physically. Emotionally, I'm drained. Let's just put it this way: Thank God I told you where I was meeting this date so the police would know where to begin their investigation. The guy was a real nutcase. Hope all is well with you. Let's talk soon. Bye."

I was thrilled to have the rest of the evening to myself. I

couldn't wait to soak in a bubble bath. I had been taking so many of them these days that my skin seemed to be in a perpetual state of shrivel. It was only in the tub that I had total seclusion. While submerged in bath oils, I reminisced about the good old days of couples. With vanilla-scented vapors wafting around me, I was in a steamy state of dream-like suspension, while I fantasized what my life might be like down the road, in a month or two . . . or even twelve.

There'd be a guy, maybe just average looking, but one whose heart and soul soared above the skies. He'd want to be with me as often as I'd want to be with him, which was almost always. He'd have kind, luminous eyes and he'd have a perpetual half-smile/half-smirk on his face, even when he was trying to be serious. He'd have a couple of grown kids, for whom he still unhesitatingly would give his life. He'd have a job he enjoyed, but one that didn't own him. He'd love to talk and he'd love to listen. He'd be very smart, spontaneous, and passionate about life. He'd cry in sad movies and he wouldn't be embarrassed. He would have a generous spirit, rarely being able to pass the man on the corner selling *StreetWise* without stopping to buy a copy of that week's edition, which he seldom read. He'd rent a corny video movie that he knew he'd hate but was just as certain that I'd love. And, best of all, he'd see humor in almost every situation, sometimes with an irreverence that was infectious, but never mean-spirited. I dipped my washcloth in the hot water and put it over my face, remembering that the guy about whom I was fantasizing had died nearly six years ago.

I got out of the tub and wrapped a towel around me, walked into the living room, turned on my CD player, hit the SHUFFLE button and pressed PLAY. One minute Placido Domingo was singing from Bizet's *Carmen* while the next, Van the Man was crooning to his brown-eyed girl with Joni Mitchell somewhere in the middle, begging Carey to get out his cane. The SHUFFLE was my favorite feature. I loved its spontaneity. It was about as impetuous and impulsive as my life had been these past few years.

As this musical anticipation was taking hold of me, I reached for the safer photo album that was on top of my credenza. It was the one with the paisley-printed cover that held pictures from the mid-sixties. I sat down on the floor and carefully began to turn the pages. Oh, my God. Look at that hair. What was I thinking? And what was my *mother* thinking, letting me leave the house with hemlines that barely covered my ass? She no doubt was out shopping the day that picture was taken. Oh, no. Here was one of our high-school singing trio. I still have that guitar somewhere. It cost fifteen dollars, and I clearly remember that I only had eight and my sister, Connie, without equivocating, gave me the other seven. It was 1964 or '65, I think. I was a good kid, but definitely a non-conformist. Here was another taken with my first boyfriend. He was tall and skinny and played the bongo drums, a few years ahead of his time. I thought that he was the coolest guy in our otherwise square eighth grade class.

I did most of my growing up in the sixties. I had a fake ID and went to my first nightclub when I was fifteen to see the new folk singing idols who were making their Chicago debut. Although it would be years later before we would learn that Peter, Paul & Mary were doing drugs and dating minors, it wouldn't have mattered to me a bit. Their songs were making statements and shaping history.

Fast forward. Meet Jeff.

Like me, Jeff was a child of the sixties. And also like me, his email said that he went to "that little red schoolhouse in Madison," the university that earned the title because it was the hotbed of liberalism. Married once and divorced for the past thirteen years, Jeff was a psychologist at a junior high school in the suburbs.

Jeff revealed his last name to me, something one generally does not do during cyber courtship. He said that his real surname was Griffin, but he had legally changed it years ago. I immediately concluded that not only was he running from the law for some heinous crime he had committed, he was about to spontaneously confess to me online. I've been known to unintentionally draw things out of people. Thankfully, I was wrong.

Jeff said that he and his ex-wife, Jackie, met in college and were engaged by their senior year. Neither wanted to take the other's last name. They wanted to free themselves from convention. They wanted to be unencumbered by societal mores and equitable to one another. And they loved nature. So, a few months before they married, they went down to City Hall and legally changed their last names to "Wilderness." Jeff and Jackie Wilderness. Soon-to-be Mr. and Mrs. Wilderness. They had a small ceremony, Jeff said. Just Jackie's parents and about a half dozen of their friends. Jeff's parents, Mr. and Mrs. Griffin, refused to come to the ceremony. If their name wasn't good enough for their son and new daughter-in-law, then they wanted no part of the wedding. Jeff and his ex had two children. A boy, Leif, and a girl, Tawny.

According to Jeff, their marriage was solid for more than twenty years. Then, one day Jeff became ill at work and went home early. Apparently, he walked in on Mrs. Wilderness rolling in the hay with one of their neighbors. Jeff filed for divorce a month later. So much for "Make love, not war," I thought. Jeff related all of this to me in one of the longest, most exhausting, introductory emails I had ever received. Jeff and Jackie Wilderness. What in the world had they been thinking, I thought to myself? And, perhaps more to the point, what drugs had they been taking? Although I assumed Jeff did not intend to be humorous, I found this most amusing and wanted to meet this guy. So, we made a date to get together for a drink at a little bar called Sid's Lounge. Jeff posted no picture with his profile, but he described himself as slim, about five-foot-eleven, very youthful looking, with silver hair and green eyes.

I walked to Sid's, which was about a half mile from my home. When I arrived, I looked around and saw no one but a few servers and a bartender. I had the place all to myself, so I ordered a glass of Merlot (I was feeling daring and, besides, red was healthier) and took it to a small table in the back. I no sooner removed my jacket, than I looked up and saw a man at the door with shoulder-length, white hair coming toward me. He was wearing a faded blue tunic shirt, a pair of jeans, and scruffy brown leather boots that looked as old as he. He had a small silver ring in one earlobe, beads hanging around his neck, and he was carrying a black leather jacket over his shoulder.

"Francine?" he asked.

"Jeff," I replied.

I extended my hand to shake his, although the thought did occur to me that perhaps I simply should have flashed him the peace sign. He shook my hand and sat down.

"Good to meet you, Jeff," I said. "How are you?"

"I am beat," Jeff said. "I saw five students today. Man, every one of them is really screwed up."

"Oh, that's right, you're a school psychologist. Must be interesting work," I said.

"It'd be a lot more interesting if I didn't have to deal with these kids' parents, a bunch of money-grubbing Republicans," he went on.

This was going to be at least a two-drink evening, I said to myself.

"How do you know they're all Republicans?" I asked, not wanting to discuss politics on the first date. Besides, I already had a sense that Jeff's political views were somewhere to the left of Ho Chi Minh.

"How do I know? Oh, let me paint the scene. The mothers drop their little darlings off at school in their brand new Beemers or Mercedes before they take their husbands to the train station. Then they head over to Starbucks for a grande cappuccino and a quick read of *The New York Times.* Then it's off to the club for a tennis lesson and a light lunch with their girlfriends, after which they go get their hair or nails done, run to the day spa for a massage, make another quick stop at Starbucks for an iced vanilla skim latte before picking up their kids at three."

Call me crazy, but this lifestyle was sounding great to me.

"So when do you interact with these parents?" I asked, looking into Jeff's burned-out eyes.

"Every seven or eight weeks, when the grades start coming out. Of course, if the kids are getting As and Bs, I don't hear from their parents much. But when they start pulling down Cs and

Ds, then the kids must be troubled, because they couldn't be just dumb. So that's when the parents come in to see me. 'Why aren't I reaching their kid's inner child? Why can't I help Johnny to focus?' Let me tell you, it's hell."

"I'll tell you hell, Jeff. I was a former high school teacher in Chicago's inner city in the seventies, before the days of metal detectors. On my first day of class one school year, a fourteen-year-old kid pulled out a gun and shot another student in the hallway. Fortunately, the victim didn't die. But I almost did—of a heart attack. They dismissed everyone early that day, and security escorted all of us teachers to our cars. I drove home, shaking all the way. I stuck it out in that school for a few years, until I decided to make a career change. Now, *that's* hell," I blurted out. I then took a deep breath and a big gulp of my Merlot.

God, I didn't know where this tirade came from. I didn't mean to be confrontational. It wasn't my nature. But I wanted to reach over and slap Mr. Wilderness. I wanted to take this aging hippie and get him to Tune In to reality, Turn On to alternatives, and Drop Out of the profession if he hated it so much. I had a very bright, well-educated, unemployed friend who'd been job hunting for over a year who would have traded places with Jeff in a second.

Jeff called the waitress over and ordered a beer. He looked uncomfortable sitting upright in his chair. Perhaps he was missing the days of lounging in a conversation pit.

"So how long have you been a psychologist?" I asked sweetly, trying to compensate for my mini outburst.

"Too long. Actually, I had my own practice for about three years after grad school, but I couldn't make ends meet. Not enough patients. So, I took this school gig in the seventies to get regular hours and bennies. Then, two years ago, I really needed a break so I took a twelve-month leave of absence before coming back."

"A whole year off. Did you travel? I've always fantasized about taking a chunk of time off to do some real traveling through Europe."

"No, I haven't done much foreign travel. Although I was in Tijuana once."

"So what did you do on your leave of absence? Write?"

"No, I trucked," he mumbled, as he swigged his Corona.

"You what?" I asked, not understanding his garbled remark—ready to feel offended.

"I went to work as a trucker. I traveled mostly through the Midwest, although I did have a big delivery down in El Paso once. Actually, that's where I dropped off the truck . . . in Texas. Hung out with an old college buddy of mine for about a week. Man, did we have a blast. Talked about old times every night until about two in the morning. But I could tell that his wife was getting really pissed. So, at the end of the week, I split. I bought a motorcycle and rode it back to Chicago."

I could almost hear the theme song from *Easy Rider*. Maybe Jeff could change his last name again, this time to "Hopper."

"Do you still have the motorcycle?" I asked.

"You bet. I ride it every Sunday."

"To church?" I was having fun, now.

"No. I'm in a cycle group. We go to places like Champaign, Kenosha, South Bend. Last weekend, we rode all the way to Madison, Wisconsin, to see Cher's farewell concert."

"How was it?"

"She was okay, but her opening act was better. Cyndi Lauper. You know, 'Girls Just Wanna Have Fun.' And let me tell you, there were lots of girls up in our old stomping grounds who still wanted to have fun. Boy, Madison brought back great college memories. Like marching on Bascom Hill and sitting in at the Union to protest the speaking engagement of Strom Thurmond. Who'd ever think that that ol' fart would live that long. Another right-wing racist. And the Big Burn. God, that was awesome."

"The big what?" I thought that maybe Jeff had spent too much time out on Lake Mendota without sunblock.

"The Big Burn. You know, the collective burning of our draft cards. That's something I'll never forget. Hey, listen, would you like to ride up to Madison with me sometime, Francine? It only takes about three hours on my cycle. It's way too cool up there."

Here we were: Mr. and Ms. Polar Opposites. Jeff was referring to the atmosphere, as I was recalling the temperature.

"Gee, thanks for the invitation, Jeff, but my back would never survive the trip." Nor would my mind, without hallucinogens, I thought. "Jeff, I've got to get up early tomorrow. I have about a twelve-hour day at work. It was nice meeting you. Maybe we'll run into each other again sometime," I said. Like at a Timothy Leary convention, I thought to myself.

"Yeah, Francine, I'd better get going, too. Big day for me tomorrow. I have to see four students."

Four students, I thought. Where can I sign up?

We shook hands again and as I walked home, I started to recall my own hippie days. Bandanas around our heads, tie-dyed halter tops, bare feet, macramé ankle bracelets, long hair on girls, longer hair on boys, going braless, antiwar protests, sit-ins, knowing every word to Joan Baez and Bob Dylan songs as we strummed our guitars. Hard to believe that that was over thirty years ago. It was a wild and fun time, but it's over. Don't get me wrong. I still love the past and reflecting on my college days. Discovering for the first time some of the brightest minds in literature and in life . . . pulling group all-nighters . . . sipping endless cups of coffee and puffing Pall Malls, while banging out that term paper with the extra-wide margins on the old Olivetti. But, as with most stages of my youth, I outgrew it. Maybe Jeff will, too, someday, I thought. And when he does, maybe we could try to meet again. On second thought, I'll be dead by then.

I got home and headed straight for my bubbles. While soaking in the tub, I thought about Jeff. Would I have accepted the date with him if he had posted his picture and I had seen, in advance, his shoulder-length hair, earring, and beads? Maybe, maybe not. Actually, I didn't regret the date, after all. It was interesting and it was a diversion.

For the rest of the evening, I wondered about Jeff and his obsession with the past. He certainly seemed to delight in reminiscing about his college days, almost to the point of re-creating them. And, as I thought about my own Beetle-load of great things to remember, I admitted that it was fun for one night. But I think I figured out why Jeff was so stuck in yesterdays. Comfort. It was his safety zone. Looking forward can trigger an anticipatory anxiety attack. These memories were familiar. And familiarity didn't breed contempt here. It fostered a safe feeling. A real sense of security. A protected place where he—we—could dwell.

Time to shelve those memories or, at the very least, compartmentalize them, Jeff.

Time to let go, Francine.

16

Mike

WHEN I WAS FIVE years old, I went to my best friend, Annie's, birthday party. Annie invited about ten other kindergartners, all of whom arrived with presents, some elaborately wrapped in foil paper, others covered in white tissue, tied with curled, colored ribbon. I walked into the party with the birthday card that I had picked out all by myself. I remember the card to this day, because it had a picture of a little girl on the front, playing with a puppy. Throughout my childhood, I had wanted a dog more than anything in the world, but my father could never understand the concept of bringing live animals into one's home, having come from a tiny European mountain village where animals who managed to get into the house were shooed out with a broom. So I tried to compensate by leashing my stuffed, toy dog and taking him for a walk down the street when I was four (until some older kids teased me mercilessly), pinning my pigtails up with plastic puppy barrettes, borrowing library books about dogs, collecting ceramic canines of every breed, and having dogs in every picture I drew and on every greeting card I bought.

My mother watched, as I painstakingly signed Annie's birthday card. Then she took it from me, placed something in it, and sealed it in its pale-pink envelope. She tied a ribbon around the envelope and made a beautiful bow and, as she handed me the card, she said, "Franny, your gift will be the best present of all—one that the birthday girl will never forget."

Who was I to mistrust my mother?

When it came time for Annie to open my present, a coupon fell out of the card. Being only five, Annie couldn't read what it said, so she handed it to her mother who read aloud, "'This entitles the bearer'—that's you, Annie—'to twelve ice-cream cones at Baskin Robbins.' One for every month. Oh, what a lovely gift, Annie! What do you say?"

Annie was speechless. Then she started to giggle and so did all of the other little guests. One of them blurted out, "Ice-cream cones can't fit in a card. What a stupid present!" Little did they or I know that my mother was way ahead of her time as, decades later, customers of all ages would be whipping out their music/video/book/coffee gift cards. But this was not decades later. I was only five years old and I was fighting back tears. Embarrassed to be even a tad different, I longed to go home.

Many years later—when I could bring myself to talk about Annie's fifth birthday party with my older siblings without cringing—we dubbed that experience "An Ice-Cream Story." It became our family's own personal reference to every sad encounter, crestfallen circumstance or woeful person who tugged at our hearts.

Meet Mike. Mike was a sorbet tale, at the very least. His first email to me reported that his wife had recently left him for one of her coworkers. He said that he really couldn't blame her for leaving him. Her coworker was a younger guy who resembled Mel Gibson, while he described himself as looking more like Mel Tormé.

I liked The Velvet Fog. Well, maybe not his looks, but his voice. Mike went on to say that his not-yet-ex's boyfriend had two master's degrees and was COO of the company where she worked. Apparently, while the boyfriend had been climbing the corporate ladder, Mike had been standing on a step stool as an accountant for a small firm where he had been for thirty years.

"I guess I'm just not exciting enough for her anymore, if I ever was at all. I hope I can arouse *someone's* interest out there on the Internet," his email said.

Oh, boy. I immediately thought of that cartoon character who walked around with a cloud constantly hovering over his head. I really wasn't very motivated to meet Mike for a date. But I felt sorry for him. And although I know that sympathy is not an emotion on which healthy relationships are built (I think I saw a show about that topic on *Oprah*), nonetheless, I agreed to have a drink with Mike after work the following week.

"How about Monday or Tuesday?" Mike suggested. "Those evenings usually aren't so busy for most people. I mean, I don't expect you to meet me on a weekend or anything."

This guy's self-esteem was in the basement. His wife just left him for a hunk. He was living alone for the first time in three decades. He was feeling lousy about himself. And now he thought that he was only worthy of someone's attention within the first forty-eight hours of the work week.

Francine to the rescue. I suggested that we meet on a Wednesday evening, telling him that it would be a good carrot to dangle in front of me—giving me something to look forward to in the middle of the week. Okay, I had a momentary lapse of sanity. Mike seemed elated and proposed a little piano bar that was about a half mile from my apartment. Great, I thought. I could walk on over and still be about five minutes from home.

When I arrived, there was a man standing outside of the place who appeared nervous and smelled like he had bathed in English Leather cologne. It was Mike and he was right. He did look like Mel Tormé.

"F-Francine?" he stammered.

"Hi, Mike," I said, while extending my hand. "Shall we go in?"

"Oh, definitely," he replied, holding the door open for me.

We found a little table not too far from the piano player. The server walked over to take our order.

"I'll have your house Chardonnay," I said.

"And I'll have a brandy," Mike added.

"So how was your day, Mike?" I asked.

"Oh, not good at all. I got some terrible news today," he replied.

Now, when anyone tells me they've received terrible news, my mind goes straight to health. I had lost my mother, husband, and brother in a four-year period. And although that period ended five years ago, it was still painfully fresh in my mind.

"Oh, no, Mike. What is it?" I said, swallowing and preparing myself for the worst.

"I just found out that my car is going to need $850 worth of repairs. I can't believe it. On top of everything else that's going on in my life . . . now this," he responded.

I suppose I could understand his frustration, but I don't know that I would put this in the catastrophic category. Nonetheless, I did feel sorry for the guy.

"Is it worth repairing?" I asked.

"I think so. It's a four-year-old Ford Escort with—my luck—a 36-month warranty. But it's got all the bells and whistles on it. I just love that little car," he said.

"Well, then, it's worth fixing. You know, my car is fourteen years old. The way I look at it, even with repair and maintenance bills of four or five hundred per year, I'm still ahead of the game. Who wants car payments, if you don't need them?"

"You can say that again. And I can't afford them even if I wanted a new car. When my wife left me, she told me I could have the house. It's not much of a house—three bedrooms and one and a half baths. But the mortgage payments and real estate taxes on one salary are eating me up alive."

"But you'll get a tax break at the end of the year," I said.

"I guess so, but even this average house seems too big for me now that she's gone. And then there's the upkeep. I guess I should be able to figure it out. I'm an accountant, after all, although I'm not so sure how good of an accountant I am. I was up for a promotion about a month ago. But they gave it to one of the younger, sharper guys," he said, while taking a sip of his brandy. He closed his eyes, shuddered, and made a wincing face.

"What's wrong, Mike? Are you alright?" I asked.

"Yeah, I'm fine. It's this brandy. It doesn't taste right—it's awfully bitter."

"Call our server over and ask her for something else instead," I suggested.

"No, it's okay. I don't want to cause a scene," he said, as he braced himself before taking another sip.

"So, tell me about your kids, Mike. You said that you have two boys in college." This time I had done a review of Mike's profile before meeting him.

"Yeah, they're great. Both at Big Ten schools. They have their mother's looks, thank goodness. The older one wants to go to veterinary college and the younger one wants to be a lawyer. I'll be paying for school for the next ten years or so," he added. "But that's okay. My kids are worth it. They're really going to be something someday, not like their old man."

I was starting to see thirty-one flavors. Let's see . . . I could begin with butter pecan.

"Mike, don't say that about yourself. You have a steady job. You're a loyal worker. You said that you've been at the same firm for the last thirty years. How many people can say that?" I said, trying to find something positive for him to hang onto.

"*Stuck* in the same job for the past thirty years is more like it. I started out as a junior accountant and, in thirty years, all I've accomplished is 'accountant' . . . not even 'senior accountant.' That's not a lot to show for almost one half of my life . . . a life that I used to share with someone, at least."

I didn't know how to respond. I just desperately wanted a double dip of strawberry swirl.

"Mike, is there anything else that you've always wanted to do with your life?" I asked, hoping to get him to focus on a hobby or interest outside of his profession.

"I don't know. I used to dream about being a doctor. But my parents told me that I'd never make it. And they were right. I had a hard time passing biology. For awhile, I thought about teaching, but my father said that it was a woman's profession. I always liked numbers and it seemed like the world would always need bean counters. So here I am, in a job I hate. Not like a COO of a large company, who can have any woman he wants. And the one he wants is mine," Mike went on, as his voice started to crack.

"I was talking about hobbies or pastimes. Look, Mike, you're just going through a bad period. You're at an all-time low right now. But I promise you, it'll get better. Do you have any good friends? You know, men or women you can just hang out with?"

"My wife and I had a few couples we were friends with, but they sort of vanished when she did. I guess she was the one who had all the personality. I really miss them. That's why I'm online. I'm hoping that there's someone out there for me."

"Listen. Timing is everything, Mike. You're not ready for a significant relationship yet. You're still grieving the loss of your wife. Divorce is like death, they tell me. And you need that time to mourn the end of your marriage. You also need time to take care of yourself. Get to know yourself a little better. Find out what *Mike* wants and doesn't want. It's taken me about five years to get to know myself, and I'm still learning. That's what you should concentrate on . . . not frantically searching for your perfect match. Does that make sense?" I said, as I immediately understood how much sense it made to me.

"I guess so. But that house is just so lonely, Francine. And it's hard being by myself."

"I know, Mike. But you're not really by yourself. You're *with* yourself. And there's a big difference."

"Francine, could we get together again sometime?"

Here comes rum raisin, I thought to myself. Although I didn't know him well, Mike seemed like a genuinely nice guy and good person. But we were at opposite ends of life-after-a-lifetime relationship. He was just beginning to painfully experience that stage of life while I was becoming comfortable with it.

"Mike, I'm pretty busy right now, trying to find out what *I'm* all about, too. And believe me when I tell you that we're at very different places in our lives at the moment. What you need to do right now is to spend some time with your best friend."

"I don't have one."

"Yes, you do," I said.

"No, I really don't," he insisted.

"Yes, you do. *You're* your best friend. I'll tell you what. . . . You can email me anytime. I'm a good talker. I'm a good listener. And I like writing to my friends. And we can be friends, right? So, if you need to talk to someone, I'm just a click away. Remember that, okay?"

"I will. I don't know why I'm so exhausted, all of a sudden. I'm going to try to turn in early tonight. You're a sweet person—and smart, too," he went on.

"Thanks, Mike, but I can't even add without a calculator. Experience has made me a little wise, that's all. Hang in there. And we'll talk in cyberspace soon, alright?"

"Okay. I'll email you again, Francine. I have lots of time this weekend. You'll probably be too busy to check your emails over the weekend, but it can wait until Monday," Mike said.

"No matter how hectic things are, I always check my emails on Sunday nights. Take care, Mike," I said as I got up, patted his arm and, for the first time that evening, caught a glimpse of a smile on his face.

As I headed home, I walked past a small grocery store but then, remembering that I needed a few things to get me through the week, I turned back and went in. I wanted to buy a newspaper, some juice, a quart of skim milk, and a few bananas. And maybe just a pint or two of Cherry Garcia.

I thought about Mike the rest of that night. He'll be alright, I said to myself. This is just so new to him, poor guy. It had been foreign to me once, too. Married forever and then suddenly single. A friend described that abrupt loss like someone ripping her arm right out of its socket. For me, it wasn't an arm. It was a constant knife in my stomach. On really bad days, the knife would be twisting. I realized that it had been quite awhile since I'd felt that stabbing pain.

The gnawing I was feeling right now was hunger. I walked into my kitchen, grabbed a bowl off the shelf, and opened the pint of Ben & Jerry's. Looking at the flavor's name on the carton, I couldn't help but recall that old Grateful Dead line: "What a long, strange trip it's been!"

17

Stephen

THIS TRIP *WAS* BECOMING long and strange, and the itinerary was difficult to predict. Would the next place be a great destination, filled with awesome sights, or would it turn out to be another ho-hum location, similar to somewhere I had visited before? Although I was getting better at quickly deciding what kind of settings I preferred, I was never adept at reading maps. So I simply decided to stay on for the ride. All aboard. Next stop: Stephen.

Stephen emailed me and suggested that we get together for a drink. After thoroughly reviewing his profile, I accepted. One of the great things about Internet dating—or the sizing up that precedes the dating—is that you can linger over one's profile before making up your mind. You can read and reread it as many times as you want before replying, if at all. You can get up, walk away from the computer screen, make yourself a sandwich, take a bath, catch a nap, and then return whenever the Internet spirit moves you. You can maximize a candidate's posted photo and, if that isn't sufficient, you can get out a magnifying glass and hold it up to your computer screen to see if that's a smudge on your monitor, his forehead, a Gorbachev-like birthmark, or if he's a good

Catholic who chose to post a picture of himself that was taken on Ash Wednesday.

Back to Stephen, who was cute, bald, and had a pleasant smile. He seemed to come in twos: he had two grown children, his profile stating that neither was living at home; he lived in a two-story house in the suburbs; he had two siblings; both parents were still living; and he was twice-divorced. Quite symmetrical, I thought.

Stephen was a corporate attorney who was semi-retired. He only took a case—or probably two—when they seemed interesting. He liked to golf (I wasn't about to make that mistake again), and he had a quick wit. After reading between the lines for hints of John Wayne Gacy or Hannibal Lechter and finding none, I agreed to meet him at a neighborhood restaurant on North Avenue for a drink.

I was becoming much more relaxed about these dates. No double dose of Clinique's High Impact Lemongrass eye shadow. No dragging the heavy artillery make-up bag to the office with me so that I could do an overhaul in the ladies room before leaving my nine-to-five job to set out on what used to feel like my second one. I was beginning to convince myself that if these guys were the type that I'd be interested in at all, then they'd see beyond the dual absence of freshly polished nails and big boobs. If these matches were meant to be, then they'd just happen—with a little help from my two friends: light blush and lip gloss.

I was the second to arrive at the restaurant, Stephen already sitting at a highboy table with a Scotch on the rocks. He was a fairly well-preserved late fifty-something, who greeted me with a grin and a handshake.

"Hi, I'm Stephen. You must be Francine," he said. "What are you drinking?"

"I'll have a vodka and tonic," I replied, surprisingly abandoning my sommelier aspirations.

"How are you, Francine?" he asked, convincing me that his interest was genuine.

"I'm fine. How are you, Stephen? And what brings you to Internet dating?" I asked, getting right to the point.

"Well, I'm living out in the suburbs, which definitely limits one's social life, or at least it does mine. I'm the only single on my block and I definitely subscribe to the thou-shalt-not-covet-thy-neighbor's-wife commandment. And even if I didn't, there are too many NRA-type husbands in my neighborhood who, I'm sure, are armed and somewhat dangerous," he laughed.

"Why don't you just move into the city? Not that that instantly throws you into a social whirl, but it might accelerate things a bit," I said.

"Because of my kids. They're in college, living with their mother during the summers, and I like to be close by in case they spontaneously want to get together. Of course, that hasn't happened much since they've been out of high school. Anyway, that's how I got started with this online dating thing. I figured I could use some help," he replied.

"Any luck?" I asked

"Depends upon how you define luck. No offense. I don't mean that in the typical guy sense. But I guess you could say that I've met some pretty nice women on the Internet, and I'm interested in meeting more of them," he replied.

"Increase your odds, so to speak?" I said.

"Odds . . . what do you mean?"

Oh, God. I realized that my naive question must have seemed pretty desperate: Increase your odds of finding *the one*, prince/princess charming, your soul mate, your future spouse.

"Well, I just meant the more women you meet online, the better chance you have of finding a long-term relationship with one of them," I said, a bit embarrassed.

"Assuming that's what I'm looking for," Stephen replied, with a smile.

We ordered another round of drinks and talked about our backgrounds, which really were quite similar. Stephen was raised on the south side of the city and went to Catholic elementary and high schools, before going off to the University of Michigan. A north-sider, I shared my survival of thirteen years of college-prep, parochial schools, and we compared notes on nuns from hell.

We laughed and I couldn't remember when I'd had such a good time.

About two hours later, Stephen asked if he could drive me home. I told him that I had driven myself, as a way to avoid getting into a car with a stranger, as the good sisters warned us girls never to do. In fact, I felt comfortable enough to tell Stephen about my online dating routine: that I had left word with a friend of where I'd be meeting him, what time, and approximately when to expect my "got home safely" phone call.

"You know, you gals really have it bad. Guys don't ever have to think about anything like that. We just make a date, show up, enjoy ourselves—or not—and go home," he said.

"You've obviously never seen *Fatal Attraction* or *Black Widow*. There are a few wacko women out there, too, you know," I teased.

"Right. But speaking of odds, those are pretty slim," he retorted.

Stephen called our waitress over, paid the bill, stood up, and helped me on with my jacket. I began to feel awkward. It was the "good-bye" moment, and I wasn't quite sure if there was going to be a next time. I liked this man. I mean, it wasn't as if we had learned everything about each other in the past few hours, but I wanted to get to know him better. At the very least, what I hoped for was that there would be a second date.

"Francine, maybe we could do this again, sometime. I'll call you, if that'd be okay."

"That would be wonderful," I said, perhaps too anxiously.

We exchanged phone numbers. One of the primary Internet dating rules is one of the same ones that applies to life: You Must Learn to Trust Your Gut. And mine told me that, in this case, it was perfectly safe to give Stephen my home phone number. We walked out of the restaurant, shook hands, and retreated to our respective cars.

When I got home, I almost forgot to call Linda to tell her that I had made it back, unharmed. She quizzed me about the evening, and I told her that I had a great time. It was true. I was relaxed with Stephen in a way that I hadn't felt with any of my other Internet dates. I attributed that to his easy-going demeanor. Or maybe I was simply becoming more comfortable on these journeys.

Three days lapsed, but no call from Stephen. A week . . . and then two more. Then, one evening almost a month later, I came home from work to find my answering machine's message light blinking. I pushed PLAY.

"Is this the love of my life, Francine? It's Stephen. How are you? I was wondering if you'd like to get together on Thursday night. Maybe we could have dinner. Call me."

Where was *The Rules* when I needed to reread it? It was Monday. Do I call him back tonight? Do I wait until Tuesday? Wednesday would be too late to make a date for the following night. Should I blow him off altogether? After all, did he think I was going to be sitting around for a month, just waiting by the phone?

I called him the next evening and got his voice-mail.

"Hi, Stephen. It's the love of your month, I mean life," I said coyly into his answering machine. "I'm not free this Thursday, but I would enjoy seeing you again. So give me a call—and a little more notice next time—and maybe we can get together. Bye."

It wasn't a lie. I had made tentative plans with one of my girlfriends to see a movie on Thursday night. And the cardinal rule that may or may not be in *The Rules*, because I can't remember, is that you *never* break a date with one of your girlfriends to go out on one with a guy. Period.

About six weeks went by and I had almost forgotten about Stephen—except that I hadn't, because I occasionally checked to see if his profile was still online. I found that it was. But what I didn't find were any new emails or voice-mails from him. Then, two weeks later, I came home from the grocery store to a flashing light and a new phone message . . . from Stephen.

"Hi. Is this the love of my life, Francine? It's Stephen. Listen, are you free next Tuesday? I thought that maybe we could catch a bite to eat, or at least a drink. Call me and let me know."

Damn. I was busy on Tuesday. I had signed up for a financial planning seminar with three other women from work. I toyed with the idea of canceling it, but I didn't want to. It was important to me.

I called Stephen and, once again, got his answering machine. "Hi, Stephen, it's the love of your life. Now, in case you're confused, it's Francine. Hey, you're like a quarterly statement. It's been a while since I've heard from you. Yes, I'd like to get together but, no, I can't make it this coming Tuesday. So please try me again, okay? I mean it. Bye."

On Tuesday evening, my three coworkers and I went out to dinner before the seminar. I knew these women only casually as they were from different departments than mine. We talked about our jobs, our kids, divorce, the world of dating, how difficult it was to meet quality men. We actually discovered that we had a lot in common.

One of the women, Sarah—a beautiful woman who looked like she was in her early forties—leaned in, lowered her voice and said, "Well, ladies, I began a new adventure about two months ago: Internet dating. And I've been having a lot of fun. It's just so good to have something to look forward to when you go home at night, even if it's only on your computer screen," she went on.

"Have you gone out on any interesting dates?" another asked.

As I waited for Sarah's answer, I began to get nervous. What if Sarah had perused other women's photos online, just to see what the competition looked like, and recognized mine. Oh, no, it would be all over the office that I was an Internet dater. Then, I realized it was really no big deal, which was a huge step for me.

"As a matter of fact, I have. Last week, I had a drink with this great guy. He's an attorney, divorced, with two grown kids. He lives in the suburbs to be near them, but he works part-time in the Loop, so we met downtown one evening after work. I like him. He's laid back, with a dry sense of humor. I mean, we don't know each other that well, but the other night he left me the cutest message on my machine. He opened with, "Hi, is this the love of my life, Sarah?"

"'Love of my life?' That sounds like it could be serious," one of the other women said.

"No, he was just having fun, which is fine with me. I'm not looking for anything heavy," Sarah went on.

I'll admit I was feeling a tiny tinge of pain. Stephen was dating lots of women. Not that there's anything wrong with that, as Seinfeld would say. Timeshare romance just wasn't for me. I'm sure that Sarah, however, wouldn't have a problem with it, having admitted that she wasn't searching for anything serious. Of course, Sarah was about a dozen years younger than I, which meant that she had that much longer to *get* serious.

That was what stung. The harsh realization that there were millions of charming, eligible women out there who were much more casual about dating. Many, like Sarah, who *did* have those perfectly polished fingernails and ample breasts. Intelligent women with interesting careers. Many who had the whole attractive package. And then there was Stephen. Stephen, who obviously hadn't even fallen head over heels in *like* with Francine.

I took copious notes at the financial seminar. I had a lot of planning to do. This trip may have been strange, but who knew how much longer it was going to be? And I was definitely on board for the duration.

18

Louis

AN OLD COLLEGE FRIEND and her husband were passing through Chicago, and I met them near the airport for dinner. We reminisced about our freshman days on campus, looked at old photos, talked about our kids, knocked off a bottle of wine, and laughed till we cried. It was one of the best evenings I could remember, a real diversion. And I didn't even notice once that we were a threesome. Perhaps I was making progress.

The next day was Thursday and it was back to reality. Between the previous night's over-indulgence and an unbearable day at the office, I came home exhausted, grabbed a handful of cashews from my kitchen cabinet, and climbed into the tub with an ice water and *The New York Times*. I was swamped at work and home wasn't much better. I hadn't opened my mail in a week. I hadn't paid a bill in two. I wanted to check in with my kids. I needed a haircut. And I had no groceries in the house save a few apples, some roasted soy nut butter, and a jar of raspberry jam. All I needed to complete the eccentric-old-lady profile were seven cats running around my condo and a pile of newspapers dating back a few years. Things were starting to slip out of my control.

I walked into my therapist's office for the first time seven years ago. I began going when Bob became ill. I didn't know how to handle his illness and I had a foreboding feeling that our lives were about to change dramatically. I was right. And here I was, years later, still seeking help to adjust to the lost and found: my husband and my single status.

It was only in my shrink's office that I didn't have to play any roles. It was only here that I felt totally protected. I didn't have to be the omnipresent mother, albeit of adult children but, still, my offspring. I didn't have to dispense advice when, in reality, I wasn't always sure if my own recommendations were something I'd follow myself. I didn't have to be the professional executive, making the right decisions at the appropriate moment. I didn't have to be the wise mentor of less experienced staff, walking them through scenarios, helping them to arrive at the answers. I didn't have to be the best friend to a few women and men while they discussed their lousy marriages, extramarital affairs, mothers-in-law, grown children moving back home, dead-end jobs, and unfulfilled lives. I didn't have to be the understanding neighbor to mine while she lamented about her furniture delivery that was late or her over-priced decorator. I didn't have to be the merry widow who tried to smile while keeping up with old friends—mostly couples. And I didn't have to be the Internet dater with the mysterious identity, trying to find the one guy in cyberspace who would be my perfect match, when I was beginning to catch on that that guy probably didn't exist, at least not in this life. My therapist's office was the one place where I could let my guard down and be myself. I remembered a comment that my daughter made a few days after Bob's funeral. She turned to me and said, "Mom, you were always the glue, and now it looks like the glue is coming unstuck." In a therapist's office, it's okay to come unglued.

It wasn't until I got out of the tub that I realized I hadn't turned on my computer once since Monday. I figured I'd better check my emails, as Mike and I had exchanged some "I'm okay, you're okay" cyber chats over the previous week. No, nothing new from Mike. That was a good sign. Wait, here was one from "Louie, Lou-*eye*." Who the hell was he? Oh, right. I forgot I was still trolling. Even though I was dead tired, I decided to pull up his profile and check him out. Another advantage of Internet dating is that you can be munching noisily on cheese and crackers or a crunchy carrot stick while wearing flannel pajamas and fuzzy slippers with your hair in a ponytail and Clearasil on the tip of your nose and still have a perfectly polite, dignified conversation with a potential cyber mate.

Louis was a personal injury attorney who had lived in Chicago all of his life. I took this with a modicum of encouragement. At least we had several things in common: a love for the city and a love for justice . . . what a stretch. He invited me to meet him one night during the week. I wasn't sure I could do it. I truly was beginning to suffer from Chronic Meeting Fatigue Syndrome, doubtful that I could bear many more evenings after work of scrunching my hair with mousse, applying a second coat of lip gloss and blush, and trying to decide which captivating stories of my life I would tell to a total stranger this time. I had heard myself repeat these interminable tales dozens of times over the past three-quarters of a year, and I was beginning to make myself ill. Nevertheless, Louis sounded somewhat interesting, so I thought I'd give it a chance.

The only time that worked for us over the next several weeks was a Thursday evening. And because even that night had only a small window for both of us—six to eight o'clock—I broke my own rule and agreed to meet Louis for dinner. True, these dinners were often drawn-out disasters, but a girl's got to eat. And if this Internet dating routine did nothing else for me, it taught a former slower-than-molasses diner how to chow down in less than twenty minutes.

Louis had called me on my cell phone on Monday afternoon to make the arrangements of where and when to meet. For some reason, I didn't feel comfortable giving him my unlisted home phone number so soon, but a cell was different. It offered anonymity in a pin-me-down world.

Louis sounded nice enough, seemed to have a good sense of humor, and appeared to be bright in the three minutes that we spoke over the phone. He invited me to dine with him at his private club in the northern suburbs. His invitation was a generous one, but I didn't want to drive all the way out to the boonies to meet a total stranger. Surprisingly, I no longer was vying for the title of Miss Most Likely to Accommodate, as I suggested instead that we meet at any place of his choice, as long as it was in the city. Apparently, I was competing for Miss Compromise instead.

"You pick the restaurant, Louis. I only ask that it be somewhere near downtown. You work in the Loop, don't you?" I asked.

"Yeah, sure. Okay. I'll come straight from the office then. How about the Athena Restaurant on Halsted at six-thirty?" he suggested.

"Fine. I'll see you there this Thursday at six-thirty. Bye," I replied and pressed the cell's off button.

I didn't give this date much thought during the next few days. In retrospect, I think that was a healthy sign. I was making progress. I was getting less anxious about these first encounters. After all, these men were only human—most of them, anyway. And it was only an hour or so of my time. These encounters no longer seemed like the beginning of a new chapter in my life, but rather a short, hopefully insightful, paragraph or two.

I was running late on Thursday evening, as I pulled up to the Athena and jumped out of the car, leaving my keys in the ignition for the valet parker. I was walking into the restaurant when I heard a few people gasp. I turned around and witnessed a man on a bicycle who had just ridden into the side of my Toyota. I walked back over to the car and winced at the newest dent in the driver's door.

The man on the bicycle was unscathed. They sure don't build cars the way they used to, I thought to myself. But, then again, this fourteen-year-old wonder had served me well and was not about to win any prizes for looks, even before this latest impact. So I shrugged my shoulders, shook my head, watched the cyclist as he sheepishly peddled away, and walked into the restaurant.

There was a guy standing in the doorway who said, "Francine?"

"Louis?" I answered.

"Listen, I saw the whole thing. You were being helped out of the car when the guy on the bike rammed into you, weren't you?"

"No. If you saw the whole thing, then you must have seen me heading into the restaurant when he hit my car," I replied.

"Francine, if we say you were getting out of the car, this will be good for at least ten or fifteen bills. The valet service has to be responsible. You take a few days off of work for minor whiplash—or, at the very least, mental distress. Okay?"

"Not okay. I wasn't within five yards of the guy when his bicycle ran into the car door. Look, it doesn't make me happy, but it's an old car and I'm tired. Can we go in and have dinner now?" I asked, not feeling very hungry all of a sudden.

"Suit yourself," Louis said, as he led the way inside, suit being one of his favorite words, I suspected.

We sat in a booth in the back of the restaurant, and the waiter came up to our table and took our drink order.

"I'll have a glass of Rodytis," I said, breaking the white wine habit. I didn't care who I spilled red wine all over. Although, I'm sure if it stained Louis' trousers, he'd hold me liable.

"I'll take a Cutty on the rocks," said Louis.

"So, how was your day at the office, Louis?" I asked. And how many people did you cheat in the past eight hours, I thought.

"It was okay. I'm working on a case with this fucking client who is really getting on my nerves. I was all set to file a suit on his behalf a week ago, and now he's getting cold feet. He stands to make a killing, if he'd just listen to me. Some people are so fucking stupid."

"What's the case about?" I asked, my curiosity piqued.

"Well, I shouldn't be telling anyone, but I won't mention names. This guy takes the train in every day from the suburbs to his office in the Loop. And one particular day a few weeks ago, he's getting off the train, juggling his briefcase and a cup of Starbucks, and the heel of his shoe gets caught on one of the steps and he slips and falls from the train onto the platform. Another guy stops to help him up, and offers to take him to the emergency room, if he wants to go. But this fucking idiot says, 'No, I'm fine.' Of course, a few hours later, his back starts to ache, and he has to go home early. A friend of his gives him my name and number, he calls me the next day, and I tell him to stay in bed with a heating pad on his back. Does he listen? No, he says he has a big presentation to make at work the next day, and he can't afford to miss it. What a fucking moron."

"Wait, are you a doctor? I thought you were a lawyer?" I asked facetiously.

"I *am* a lawyer. I was giving him good advice. He should've stayed flat on his back in bed for a few days with a heating pad or hot water bottle."

"No. He should have put ice on his back and tried to roll over on his side or stretch out on the hard floor with a few pillows under his knees. I had a bad back once, and I know all of the remedies," I said.

"Yeah, whatever. The point is he should've listened to me."

"I think I know what the point is," I replied. "Let's change the subject and order something, okay?"

"Fine, but I don't see why you seem so touchy. This is how people make a living, Francine. And this is how smart people get rich."

"And this is what drives everyone's insurance premiums through the roof," I said.

"Whatever. The guy's a fucking dope. I'm supposed to meet with him tomorrow. I told him that he has until next Monday to take my advice or he can walk right out of my fucking office."

"Let's hope he doesn't slip and fall on the way out," I mumbled.

"What did you say?"

"Never mind. I'll have your moussaka," I said to the waiter, who was standing at our table, ready to take our order.

"And I'll have your lamb chops, medium rare," added Louis.

Did I smell a trichinosis lawsuit? I can see Louis now: upset stomach, fever, muscular swelling. No, wait—that's undercooked pork. He ordered lamb. Whew.

"So, Louis, how long have you been divorced?" I asked.

"Who said I was divorced?

"You did . . . in your profile," I replied.

"I don't remember saying that. Anyway, I'm separated. Same thing. Should be free of the bitch in about another six weeks. These last few months have been a nightmare. What a slut. She was sleeping with everyone on our block, which got to be real cozy 'cause we lived on a cul-de-sac. Yet, she's taking *me* to the fucking cleaners. By the time this fucking marriage is over, it'll be a miracle if I have a fucking nickel left."

It would be a *real* miracle if he had a different adjective left to use, I thought.

"My marriage to Ms. Moron reminds me of this joke," Louis went on, as he leaned closer, lowered his voice, and took a bite of bread. "This guy brings flowers home to his wife. She sees him coming up the walk, and she says to her girlfriend who's visiting, 'Oh, no, flowers . . . you know what this means. He'll expect me to be on my back all weekend with my legs spread in the air.' And her blonde friend says, 'Why? Don't you have a vase to put them in?'"

Louis started to laugh so hard at his own joke, that he began to choke on his piece of bread. Should I give him the Heimlich and risk being sued for not administering the maneuver properly, or should I let the guy choke to death in the Athena Restaurant, thus giving his still-wife-and-soon-to-be-widow the legal right to sue the owner? What's a girl to do? As he continued to turn blue, I whacked him on the back and he started to cough and regain his normal complexion. Although blue actually was his signature color.

"Gee, thanks, Francine. For a minute there, I thought I was a goner." And with that, he belched at the very moment that the waiter had arrived with our food, sending his compliments to the chef before he had even tasted a bite.

"So, how many kids do you have?" I asked. And did you sue

the doctor who delivered them, as it must have been the birth trauma that prevented them from scoring a perfect 1600 on their SATs, I thought.

"I have two. A son who's getting his law degree from Loyola and another son who's in medical school at University of Michigan. I told the older one to hurry up and finish law school so he can handle his brother's malpractice insurance. What a fucking racket."

"I agree," I said with a smile.

During dinner, we talked about work. His. In fact, as I look back, I'm not sure that he asked me one thing about myself. Besides, in between his stories of his clients and his off-color jokes, he was too busy mentally undressing every female who walked into the restaurant or passed by our table, including some older woman in her seventies who was celebrating her birthday with her grandchildren. An equal opportunity pig, I'll say that for him.

By the time the waiter came over to see if we wanted dessert, I was ready to bolt from the restaurant, hop into my battered car, and drive away.

"No dessert for me, thanks. I need to get going. I have a big day tomorrow," I said.

"Okay. Oh, yeah. What is it you do, again?" Louis asked.

Suppressing a smile with the straightest face I could muster, I replied, "I'm a minister. I wouldn't expect you to know. Thanks for dinner. I'll pray for you, Louis."

And with that, I stood up, shook Louis's hand, put a twenty-dollar bill on the table so he wouldn't sue me for my share, and walked out the door, wishing that I could have captured on film the confused look on his face, although it was one that I'll never forget. In fact, every time I look at that dent in my car door, I think of my dinner with Louis . . . which makes me want to drive right over to the body shop to get it fixed, even if it's not worth the repairs.

When I got home that evening, I thought of the choices I used to give my children when they were little. I never asked them "Would you like some vegetables?" What child would respond,

"Sure, pile 'em on"? I simply would ask, "Would you rather have peas or green beans tonight?" Well, these dates were starting to remind me of the vegetable choices my kids considered unpalatable. Did I want an angry man like Shelly, who was mad at the world? Or did I prefer listening to someone's forced stand-up-comedy routine, like Jack's? I could always wait ten or fifteen years for adorable Brian to grow up. Or perhaps I should take Bernie shopping for a new wardrobe before enrolling him in a basic manners course. I suppose I could consider meeting Richard or Craig again—with a body guard this time. Or maybe I'll start tie-dying my clothes and go for that spin on the back of Jeff's cycle.

No, until I found one who truly seemed to speak to my soul, perhaps I'd forego them altogether, recalling my son's response to that same question one summer evening when he was home from college and we were having dinner. "Would you like some vegetables?" I asked, while passing him a steaming bowl of broccoli. He was an adult, now, and could make his own choices.

"No thanks, Mom, I'm trying to cut back," he said wryly.

Maybe it was time for me to do the same.

19

Harry

I STAYED OUT OF THE Internet dating scene for a few months. I was tired of minutes turning into hours in front of my computer screen, only to be disappointed. Besides, I was getting more comfortable dining out or going to movies, museums, or concerts alone. I remembered my brother once saying to me that if self-conscious people only realized, sadly, how little they were noticed by others, they'd be so much more at ease. He was right. It was becoming fun, sitting alone in a corner of a restaurant, observing other customers and trying to imagine what their life stories were about. There was a newly found contentment in going to a movie and settling into a velour seat, while watching and listening to every movement and word on the screen, without having to be mindful of someone sitting beside me. Museums and galleries were overflowing with engaging people, and I found myself chatting with quite a few of them, as we'd start out as strangers but end up as acquaintances, discussing the latest exhibit for an hour or two in the organization's coffee shop.

Ironically, about a week after my last solo outing, I received Candidate Harry's email. From his first sentence, I could tell that he was smart. Very smart. Attracted to intelligent men, I responded. He commented, in somewhat of a pejorative manner, about my choice of fantasy dinner guests that I had listed in my profile, alluding to the fact that they were a disparate group. I countered that they were diverse in a positive way, and that I preferred even my *real* dinner parties to be composed of eclectic types, as it made for far more interesting conversation. His response said that I was misusing the word "eclectic." I challenged him on that one, pointing out that the word "eclectic" came from the Greek word, *eklektikos* meaning "selected and singled out." He replied that he'd bet that I hadn't seen the movie, *My Big Fat Greek Wedding* or I would have been embarrassed to make reference to an English word's Greek derivation. I told him that it was too bad that we hadn't had money on that wager, as I had seen the movie twice.

His fifth email on day two stated that he would suggest adding a few folks to my make-believe dinner party, namely Albert Camus, Francisco José de Goya, and Igor Stravinsky. This obviously was a test, one that I passed at least on name recognition, although I can't say that the latter two dudes would be high on my party list.

Exchanging emails with Harry was beginning to feel like work. Nonetheless, it was intellectually stimulating, so I agreed to meet him one evening, figuring that he'd let his defenses down in person. He suggested that we meet at Puccini's, a trendy coffee shop that played nothing but opera. No Willie's Bar for Harry.

Attached to his profile, Harry included a picture of himself, which looked like a combination of William F. Buckley and Pee Wee Herman. And if the film director Lina Wertmueller had held a side job as a beautician, *Swept Away* might have been a documentary describing Harry's coiffure. It was a well-determined wrap. Surely if he had known the destiny of his 'do, he would have insisted from the onset on being called "Harold" instead of "Harry." Alas, nicknames do have a way of sticking, unfortunately better than Harry's hair.

"The only evening that I could meet for coffee, Francine, is next Thursday," Harry wrote. "Monday evening I have a board meeting for the Alliance Française, Tuesday evening I'm going to a lecture on Molecular Technology in the twenty-first century, and Wednesday evening my book group meets at the University Club. We're discussing *The Iliad*."

Okay, Harry. I get the erudite picture, I thought to myself. Stop trying so hard to impress me. I'm busy until Thursday night myself. On Monday evening, I'm cleaning out my sock drawer, discarding all the loners, although there's an analogy there somewhere that I'd rather ignore. On Tuesday night, I'm paying bills and perusing hairstyle magazines, dog-earring pages in anticipation of my upcoming color and cut next weekend. And Wednesday night happens to be the third Wednesday of the month, which means it's checkers and cheese pizza night with my ninety-one-year-old neighbor, Virginia, who lives alone, has no relatives, and looks forward to Domino's thin crust almost as much as she does to beating me at checkers. So there's my busy, if pedestrian, schedule, Mr. Pedant.

"Well, I guess I'll be seeing you at Puccini's on Thursday evening at seven," I replied via email.

Why do people try so hard to inflate their personas? Insecurity, I suspect. And although I know that there are reasons why people do and say the outrageously phony things that they do and say, I am not a licensed therapist and I don't really care about those explanations. I am neither equipped with the credentials nor blessed with the time to analyze this and that. I'll leave analysis to Sigmund Freud and Billy Crystal. Give me face value any day.

I was the second to arrive at Puccini's on Thursday evening. Harry was the first. He was sitting at a table in the back, reading *The New York Times* book section from the previous Sunday. He was either one busy man who could not get through the entire paper in five days or this was the first time he had even laid eyes on the *Times* that week, which made me smile.

"Hi, Harry," I said, while extending my hand, only to receive a bone-crushing handshake. So much for my right hand's carpal tunnel ligament. Perhaps it's not too late to become ambidextrous, I thought. Ambidextrous, I repeated to myself . . . coming from the Latin words ambi and dexter, meaning around and right-

handed. My high school Latin teacher would be proud and, besides, I wanted to be prepared in case I was called upon by Harry
to conjugate some verbs.

"Hello, Francine," Harry said, standing up. Quite a polite man,
I thought to myself. I don't know why, but I suddenly saw him
some forty years earlier, being yanked up by his mother whenever
anyone walked into the room. He continued standing.

"Please sit down, Harry. So how has your week been so far?"
I asked.

"Unbelievably busy. My book group went over our customary
two hours. We didn't get out of the University Club until after ten.
But how can you tear yourself away from *The Iliad*?"

Oh, I don't know. After futilely trying to teach it for years to
high school students who would have preferred reading *Mad
Magazine* or anything written by Howard Stern, I never wanted to
recite another passage of it as long as I lived, I thought.

"How true. Personally, I'm reading *The Pilot's Wife*," I lied. "It's
one of Oprah's Book Club novels." I wanted to shake some of the
façade loose from Harry's person.

"I don't think I've heard of that one," he said, looking like he
had just smelled something rotten.

"No? Well, maybe you saw the made-for-TV movie. I think it
starred Melissa Gilbert. Or maybe it was Valerie Bertinelli. I always get those two confused. One's married to some big rock star.
They were just featured in *People* magazine. What's his name?"

"I really wouldn't know, Francine. I'm not into rock. And I
don't read *People* magazine."

"Oh, you should, Harry. That's how you keep up with what's
happening in the world. Or at least in Hollywood, which is just
a microcosm of the world, wouldn't you say? So what magazines
do you read?" I asked, bracing myself for a literary deluge.

"Well, I subscribe to *BBC Wildlife* and the *Smithsonian*. And I've
had a charter subscription to *Earth Island Journal* and *The Ecologist*.
And *Scientific American* and *National Geographic* are still some of
my favorites," he went on, as he picked up his coffee cup with

both hands. He looked like he was afraid that he might spill a drop or two, which surely would denote social failure.

"I love *National Geographic*," I sincerely admitted. "My parents subscribed to it for decades. I still remember when I was about seven years old, sinking into my father's enormous, black leather recliner with stacks of *National Geographic*s, longing to go to any one of the exotic destinations of the month. Even the photos that looked frightening to me—you know, tribal warriors with painted faces—were intriguing."

"I know what you mean," Harry replied. "In fact, I feel that way now. There are many places I'd like to visit, but they're so foreign and getting there seems so intimidating," he said, wistfully.

"Harry, that's what travel is all about. It's scary and exhilarating at the same time. Kind of like sex with a new partner," I went on, very out of character for me, but I just felt like Harry needed to loosen up a bit. "So what's on for your weekend?" I asked, breaking the deafening silence.

"Well, on Saturday I'm meeting an old friend for lunch. And on Sunday afternoon, I'm going to see a film at the Cultural Center. It's a documentary on wildlife in New Guinea. It's somewhere I have always aspired to visit, so this is the next best thing."

"Why don't you think about the best thing, Harry?"

"The what?"

"The *best* thing . . . not the *next* best thing. If New Guinea is someplace you've always wanted to visit, why not just go? You know, plan a vacation there."

"Oh, I don't know. It takes time to plan a trip like that. And I'm not sure about how I'd fare in that kind of climate or with a different type of diet. And then, I'd need to find someone to travel with, because I think a trip like that could be a tad daunting. Not that I'm adverse to traveling solo, but I don't know if I'd like to be so far from familiar territory all by myself."

"How about an organized tour?" I asked.

"Oh, no. I don't want to travel with a gaggle of ugly Americans. And who knows whom I might be paired with? You know, those tour groups usually have to pair people up to keep the trip affordable. I don't think I could do that. I'll be content just viewing the film on marsupials in the wild," he said somewhat sadly.

Wildlife or wild life? You decide. It seemed to me that Harry was a bag of neuroses who was hiding behind his bright mind to shield himself from interacting with the average man, not to mention from living out his dreams.

"Harry, what's the worst that could happen if you signed up for an organized tour? You could be partnered with a chronic complainer. Or maybe a non-stop talker. Or you just might be sitting next to another interesting tourist on the bus who shares the same interest in wildlife that you do. I guess what I'm saying is that life is fleeting, and then it's gone. And if you really have a dream to do something or to go somewhere, don't let anyone or anything—especially fear of the unknown—stop you. Dreams are so evanescent."

Harry answered me. I know he did, because his lips were moving. But I don't remember what his response was. I was too preoccupied with my very own awakening . . . the unforeseen advice that I was giving to myself. And my monologue wanted to catapult me out of Puccini's coffee shop and into life—*my* life—and all of the things I wanted to do, places I wanted to visit and people I wanted to see, perhaps for the last time.

I needed to work on that book I had begun almost a year ago. I wanted to write short stories about people who have touched me profoundly. Letters to my children, to be opened after I'm gone. A note to the recently retired seventy-four-year-old owner of my local dry cleaners to tell him what a wonderful family business he ran for fifty years and how the whole neighborhood misses him. I wanted to send greeting cards to the few remaining acquaintances of my mother's who still reside in the nursing home where she spent the last two years of her life, even if they wouldn't have the faintest recollection of who I was. I promised myself I'd start a scrapbook for my grandchildren who recently entered the world—with pictures of them at every stage, and captions beneath them written by their grandmother, who hoped to have many years left to get to know them.

I wanted to learn how to do the bachada. I needed to sign up for conversational French lessons and re-enroll in my Saturday morning roller-blading class, even if all of the other students were nine and ten years old. I wanted to take tai-chi and start rereading all the great classics, save *The Iliad*. I longed to travel to places, nearby and far away. To a neighborhood just two miles from mine to visit my homebound ninety-one-year-old Aunt Sophie to tell her how much I love her, although I wasn't sure she'd understand or remember me. To visit my college roommate in California whom I hadn't seen in thirty years, although we had talked about getting together for at least half of those three decades. Across the ocean to see my only living uncle who, at age ninety-six, still manages to dance when he's happy. To visit dozens of cousins living in another country . . . simply because we're cousins.

Harry was saying something about the Australian plains, when I interrupted him.

"Harry, I've got to go now. This has been the best date I've had in a long time," I said with the utmost sincerity.

"Well, thank you. It *has* been nice, hasn't it? When do you think we could meet again?" he asked, nervously.

"I don't know, Harry. But I don't think anytime soon. Not because of you. It's me. I've got a million and one things to do in the next few months. By the way, I should be the one to thank *you*. You've really made me reflect on things. That's why I've got to run now. Good-bye, Harry," I said as I stood up, put my coat on, gave him a hug—much to his surprise and mine—and headed for the door. I looked back to see a quizzical look on Harry's face, so I dashed back to the table.

"Harry, listen to me. You *must* go on that trip to New Guinea. *The Iliad* will still be here when you get back. Call a travel agent tomorrow. Or better yet, book tonight . . . online!"

I waved good-bye to him as I hurried outside. Walking to my car, I felt an unprecedented energy. I drove back to my apartment building, walked into the lobby, held up my hand, and gave my doorman the high five. He looked at me in amazement, as he said, "Good evening, Ms. Francine. Have a good one."

The elevator door opened and I stepped in. I had such an over-whelming sense of urgency that I would have taken the stairs, if not for the fact that I lived on the 37th floor. I was the only one in the elevator, as my foot nervously tapped . . . 35 . . . 36 . . . 37. The door finally opened. I dashed down the hallway with my keys in hand and quickly let myself into my apartment. I dropped my purse on the floor of my living room and walked over to the an-swering machine, its message light blinking, displaying two calls. I pressed PLAY.

"Francine, where are you? It's Nancy. Call me when you get home."

Later, I thought. I pressed DELETE.

"Hi, Francine. It's Shelly. Remember me? We haven't talked in quite awhile. I've been really busy. I've been involved in a law-suit against my ex brother-in-law, the cheating bastard. It's a long story. Maybe we could have dinner sometime soon. Call me."

"Oh, puhleeze," I said aloud. I pressed DELETE again . . . twice, just to make sure. There was no time tonight for a long soak in the tub. I showered, got out, dried myself off, and put on my green, plush, terry cloth robe—the one piece of clothing that felt the clos-est thing to someone's arms around me. I walked back into the living room with my legal pad and pen and sank into my favorite oversized chair. I looked at my watch and was relieved to see that it was still early, although I clearly felt as if I could stay up all night.

I had to start making one of the longest lists I would ever write.

20

Sweet Mandolin

THE MORNING AFTER MY date with Harry, I awoke in the same curled-up position on my chair where I had fallen asleep, pen and paper still in hand. I first thought that it was Saturday, but then reality set in and I realized it was only Friday. I got up, walked over to the dining room table, opened my briefcase, pulled out my calendar, and let out a loud "Yes!" as I noted not one single meeting. Perfect.

An hour later, I called my secretary—who always arrived at the office promptly at seven-thirty—and told her that I wouldn't be in. After reassuring her for nearly five minutes that I was feeling fine, I finally said to her jokingly, "I just need a mental health day." In truth, I needed about 365, but one was a start.

I stepped out on my balcony to a glorious October morning—crisp and sunny—the ideal combination. I went back inside and looked around my apartment, noticing that it was in dire need of a major pick-up. I was tempted, but thought to myself, "No, this is *my* day. Like *The Iliad*, the dust will still be here when I get back." Then I glanced at my computer. I could have some fun and go male shopping for a few hours. No, the computer will be here when I return, too, it being the one constant in my life. But return from where? I felt like Ferris Buehler without a concrete plan.

I quickly showered, donned my jogging togs and running shoes, and decided to explore my neighborhood. I had moved to this area precisely because of all the interesting cafés, antique shops, and bookstores that were within "spitting distance" of me, as my mother would say. But, having no intention of measuring miles by spewing from my terrace, I grabbed a pen, pad of paper, and my backpack, and headed out instead.

My first stop was an intriguing coffee shop, its entrance down a flight of stairs from the sidewalk. I often noticed that on weekends, the line of anxious patrons went up those stairs and down the block. I wondered what coffee could be so special that its customers would queue up, but I never before had the time to find out. Time was certainly mine today.

I entered the Kaffeine Klatch to find overstuffed couches and loveseats with colorful pillows, leather chairs and ottomans, and large, glass-top coffee tables with papers from all over the world — some a few weeks old — strewn on them. The clientele seemed as international and relaxed as the reading material.

A striking African man in a dashiki was sitting in an easy chair, speaking Shona or Ganda or some lilting language to his little girl, who seemed interested only in dipping her finger in her father's whipped cream, which topped his exotic-looking drink. She then took her finger and dabbed the tip of his nose, squealing with delight.

Across the room was an elderly lady partaking of a scone, which she had carefully dissected into about a half-dozen slices so as not to waste one crumb. Next to the scone sat a large, ivory-colored pot with a strainer of loose tea leaves hanging from it. She kept glancing at her watch and just as she picked up her tea, another woman walked in, rushed over to her, and said in a very British accent, "I'm terribly sorry I'm late, Edna, but Minnie went into an awful fit about my leaving. I swear that cat thinks she rules my life." Edna just shook her head and sipped her Earl Grey, which I could smell from where I was standing.

Two Asian men who looked to be in their eighties were play-ing backgammon. They were wearing soaked tee shirts that said "Tai Chi-Town." A young man in his twenties sporting a silver stud in his left brow approached me and said, "You can sit any-where you like. I'll be back for your order in a minute."

There was an entire world in here—just a few blocks from where I lived—of which I was totally unaware. I realized what a busy yet sheltered life I had been leading this past year. I went to work, occasionally saw my family, got together with a few friends, had dates with total strangers, and then I did it all over again. Was this how the majority went through their lives, I wondered? It saddened me to think so. I immediately heard my mother's voice saying, "Francine, be happy that you have your health. There are worse existences in the world, you know." Yes, I knew that. But there were better ones, too. And I felt ready for one.

It took me an hour to finish my cappuccino. I never before took such delight in swirling the cinnamon around and around with my spoon until the foam became a rich caramel color. In fact, I seldom noticed the frothy top at all, usually drinking my coffee in the car on my way to work or hurrying off to somewhere—my eyes fixed on the road—always rushing to *somewhere*.

Jared—I had heard all of the patrons call him by name—came over to me and asked if he could get me anything else or was I okay. Those actually were two separate questions, Jared, and I didn't know how to respond, so I simply replied, "No, I'm fine." He smiled sweetly, as if he knew that this was a significant day for me and handed me the check. I left a five dollar bill . . . three for the coffee and the rest for this find.

I strolled the neighborhood for at least an hour, although it seemed like only a few minutes. I noticed everything in a way I never had before. When did someone plant lilies around the mail-box on the corner? Who stenciled stars on the lantern outside the hardware store? Where did the bronze plaque on the park bench come from? As I got closer, I read the inscription: "To Ida, Who Always Will Be Sitting Right Next To Me." I looked up to see an old bearded man a few feet away, playing with a dog that looked just like him.

"A Cairn Terrier?" I asked.

The old man's face lit up and he replied, "Why, yes, how'd you know that?"

"I purchased a book on all breeds and studied it before I bought my first dog. Good thing, too. He lived to be fourteen years old."

"Let's see, now . . . that's ninety-eight in human years. Almost as old as me," he laughed. "Duke here is only two. I sure hope I live long enough to see him through his adolescence. That's a terrible stage for dogs."

"For humans, too. Where'd you get Duke?" I asked.

"From 'Canines on Clybourn.' You'd be surprised at some of the fine-looking specimens they have in there. I knew right away that Duke was the one for me because his eyes reminded me of my wife's . . . big and soft and warm. Wish I could've taken a *couple* of those pups home, but I only have room for me and Duke," he went on.

"Well, Duke's mighty lucky," I said.

"Now there's where you're wrong, young lady. I'm the lucky one," he said as he leaned over to adjust Duke's collar.

I couldn't help but think that he wanted to linger a bit and talk. It was just he and Duke, and I guessed that these outings were the high points of the day for both of them.

"I live only a few blocks away. I'm usually at work on Fridays, but I'm playing hooky today and I plan to do it more often. Keep that to yourself, okay?" I confided.

"Your secret's safe with me, madam," he said in a whisper.

"Well, I'd better run. I'll see you again. Take care, now. And, Duke, you stay out of trouble," I said as I waved good-bye to him.

I was on a mission. I wanted to visit my favorite bookstore. Beverly's was a rare species—an independent store on Clark Street among the other "B" chains. Beverly's was comfortable. There was a coffee pot on a small table in the back of the store, undoubtedly to keep up with the competition. Other than that, Beverly's was unique and, in my opinion, was the best. A bookshop without escalators and only one small computer at the front desk. A bookstore that didn't sell wrapping paper, greeting cards, flash lights, key chains, refrigerator magnets, or CDs . . . just books. What a concept!

I'd never before had the luxury of going to Beverly's on a weekday . . . only Saturdays, Sundays, and an occasional weeknight. One Thursday evening about a year ago, I heard Studs Terkel discussing his latest book at Beverly's. It was a special night in the small shop—like being in someone's living room—as this ninety-year-old man related his many life experiences with such joie de vivre, while he talked about the future as if he would go on living forever.

I'd never actually met Beverly—in fact, I wasn't even sure that there was such a person. But I always heard the other patrons and shop's employees refer to the store as "hers," as in "her guest speaker next Monday evening will be so-and-so" or "she expects to get that book in sometime at the end of next week." I could picture Beverly in my mind. She had long, gray hair that she wore flowing down her back, a la Mary Travers sans Peter and Paul. There wasn't a Peter or a Paul in Beverly's life. There never was, I was certain. Her signature dress was a gauzy, linen caftan with matching pants that stopped short of her ankles, on one of which was a beaded bracelet. There were no shoes—ever. That was *my* Beverly. In reality, if there was a Beverly, she probably was this corporate yuppie in her forties who lived on the sixty-eighth floor of the Hancock building, but you could not get me to change my image of her. I felt like we were old friends. Just like when I would go to Bloomies to buy Bobbi Brown makeup and the saleswoman would say, "Bobbi has a new lip gloss you must try. She swears by it," as if she had just lunched with her. I could see the three of us—Bobbi, Beverly, and I—meeting for a drink some night, discussing the latest books and blush.

Although I'm sure that they weren't new to Beverly's, the day staff at Beverly's was new to me. I immediately noticed an older personnel, whereas the evening crew was peppered with pierced parts and multi-colored hair. Yet they were all bibliophiles, the night staff often recommending the latest books with such eagerness that it was obvious that they truly had devoured every word. One of the employees whom I had come to know quite well was a young author named Colin who had published a book at the ripe old age of twenty-four. He sold me an autographed copy one evening along with the *Writer's Guide to Book Editors, Publishers & Literary Agents*, as I told him that I wanted to get serious about finishing a book I'd begun years before.

"This was my bible when I got started," Colin said, as if a man with years and years of experience. And when I looked into his blue-gray eyes that dominated his youthful face, I *did* see decades of events that I could only imagine. After reading his book, I later learned what some of those were: leaving home at the age of fourteen . . . living out Jackson Browne's "Boulevard" for his next hit . . . crediting an older woman in her late thirties with cleaning him up and turning his life around before he was eighteen, enrolling him in a creative writing class after she had read a few pages of his journal. And now, at twenty-four, he was something I had only dreamed of becoming: a published writer. Not a wealthy one, he pointed out, which is why he worked the night shift at Beverly's. But his days were free. Free from the streets, free from drugs, and free to pursue penning his second novel, which he had been commissioned by his publisher to do. All this living in just two-dozen years. I was awestruck and impressed.

"So, you're working on a book," he said one evening, with a most sincere grin. "What's it about?"

When I hesitated, he said, "Don't worry. I know how it is. You don't want to jinx yourself by revealing the story. I understand."

How could this young kid sympathize so perfectly, I wondered. His perception was uncanny. I had been working on a book on and off for a few years but had never revealed that fact to anyone, lest the whole project disintegrate into air, a most likely outcome, I feared.

"How's Colin?" I asked the woman behind the desk, as I

walked into Beverly's. She looked at me for a moment with a blank stare, and then said, "Oh, he's fine."

Although I'm sure that he had no idea, Colin had become an important person in my life. I'd stop in when I could see through the window that the shop wasn't busy, so that Colin would have the time to answer my most naive questions about the process of marketing one's writing—the complexities of a good query, how to narrow down the intimidating list of agents, to go or not to go directly to a publisher, what was a reasonable length of time to wait before sending sample chapters to the next name on the list, and the all-important lead.

But it was more than his answers and time that I so deeply appreciated. Colin took this middle-aged woman seriously, or so it seemed. And we could talk about anything—his fractured childhood, my stable but somewhat lonely one. His beginning his new life at eighteen—my embarking on marriage at that exact age.

Although he never asked after that one and only time what my book was about, he politely posed many other questions about my life: was I married, did I have children, what was my day job, what kinds of books were my favorites, my musical preferences and so on. We talked about the top ten best sellers. We argued the literary worth—or lack thereof, in my opinion—of science fiction. We compared screen adaptations with their novels, discussing who *we* would have cast in the leads instead. Bruce Willis as *The Bonfire of the Vanities'* Peter Fallow? All wrong, we agreed. I offered Michael Caine or Jeremy Irons. Colin countered Mick Jagger. Now that was an interesting thought, I said.

He told me about his friends—people of all ages and walks of life. He had many author and musician acquaintances, student buddies, and a few others who still lived on the streets. He told me about his girlfriend, "Staci with an 'i,'" he said with a smile, and I knew by the way he spoke her name that she was special to him.

Even when Beverly's was too busy, Colin never was—at least not so much to prevent him from looking up and saying, "How's

the manuscript coming along? I expect to see the published product one of these days."

No, Colin had no idea how he had become the link with my
present as well as my future . . . nor had I. How, indeed, his caring
comments filled my many lonely hours in such a productive way
that time began not only to fly by, but I started to look toward the
future. . . true, with a sense of anxiety, but look forward, just the
same.

It was one in the afternoon when I had walked into Beverly's.
I didn't expect Colin to be at work this early, but I asked if he was
working his usual four to eleven shift that evening.

"Colin's off today. He's taking a long weekend. Won't be in till
next Tuesday. Are you his friend who's here to pick up a copy of
Corelli's Mandolin by Louis de Bernieres that was on back order? It
came in yesterday," she said.

"I'm a friend of his, but I'm just here to browse and write. As
for Corelli's Mandolin, no, the copy's not for me. I've already read
it . . . so many times, in fact, that I even have some of my favorite
lines memorized. Colin and I spent many an hour discussing the
book. He must have ordered a copy for another friend of his. I
haven't been in for weeks. Tell him Francine said 'hi' when you see
him, will you?" I asked.

"Oh, you're Francine? He's mentioned you. I'm Mary. He was
wondering why you hadn't been in for a while. Sure, I'll tell him
you said hello. Meanwhile, make yourself comfortable. Listen,
we're going to order a pizza for lunch. Care to join us?" she asked
cheerfully.

"You know, that sounds great. I'm starving and I don't want to
break away for lunch, so count me in. Thanks," I replied. Where in
the world could you find a bookstore like Beverly's?

I found a secluded spot at the back of the shop and spread out
the contents of my backpack on a small table. A yellow highlight-
er, which went with me everywhere, although I don't have a clue
why; four ballpoint pens, and a legal pad, on which I'd scribbled
my list from the night before. I walked over to the coffee station
and poured myself a cup of decaf and brought it back to my table.

About thirty minutes later, Mary was handing me a huge slice of cheese pizza on a blue and white paper plate.

"Thanks, Mary. How much do I owe you?" I asked.

"Forget it. We always order an extra large on Fridays and end up throwing a third of it away," she insisted.

"Well, thanks, again. I'll have to take Fridays off more often," I laughed.

I don't know how long I sat there. All I know was that my pizza was long consumed, I was on my second cup of decaf and I was making progress on my manuscript. It felt so good to be writing again . . . Colin would be proud. I'd have a lot to report when I saw him next time.

I had kicked off my shoes and was looking up a word in my worn pocket thesaurus when I heard a fluid voice say, "Only a writer would bring her own thesaurus with her to a bookstore. What's the word you're looking for?"

Almost forgetting where I was for a brief moment, I looked up to see a middle-aged man with piercing blue eyes made even clearer through his wire-rimmed glasses, smiling down at me.

"Pardon me?" I asked, as I stared a bit too long at his eyes.

"I'm sorry. That was rude of me. I didn't mean to startle you or break your concentration, but you just looked so cute, engrossed in the middle of Beverly's, that I couldn't resist breaking into your world. Please forgive me."

I could feel my face become warm. A flash or a flush? Who knows? Cute was about the last thing I felt or even cared about. Oh, God, and I didn't even blow-dry my hair this morning.

"Is there really one?" I asked, somewhat flustered.

"One what?"

"A Beverly," I clarified.

"Of course. Haven't you ever met her? She comes in once or twice a month. Like Mother Goose checking her goslings, which in her case are the latest books, and then she disappears for a few weeks. I hear she's a legend in the neighborhood," he replied.

"Well, I'm still kind of the new kid on the block. I've only been living in the area about a year. I've been coming to Beverly's fairly often, but usually in the evenings, whenever I happen to have a free one," I said. Which was almost always, I thought to myself.

"I don't live in the area at all. I just like driving up to the city a few times a month and stopping at Beverly's. Do you work evenings?" he asked.

"Rarely. I work the standard nine to five, but I'm playing hooky today. How about you?" I asked.

"I'm sorry. I interrupt your writing trance and then I don't even introduce myself. I'm Peter," he said while extending his hand. "I'm a consultant who works only a few hours a week . . . about as part-time as you can get. And never on Fridays. Besides playing golf and watching sports, I'm a voracious reader, which is why I'm in here, stocking up on books to take back to my small place in the country. And your name?" he asked.

"I'm Francine. Good to meet you, Peter."

"So, *you're* Francine? Colin has told me a lot about you. In fact, you're the reason I'm here today. Well, indirectly anyway. I'm picking up this book that he ordered for me," he said, as he held up a copy of *Corelli's Mandolin*. "Colin and I were talking about relationships a few weeks ago—namely his with his girlfriend, Staci—and he couldn't believe I hadn't read it. He said that there was a customer who'd told him that the book was one of her favorites. She even had a few of its passages memorized," he went on.

"Well, I guess he was referring to me. You're in for a real treat of a read. The setting is in Greece—on the island of Kefalonia. Have you ever been to Greece?" I asked.

"No, but it's on my list. How about you?"

"Lists? Do I ever make lists! Oh, you mean Greece. Yes, I've been there many times. I have lots of relatives in Greece and each time I've gone, I usually wind down my trips on one or two islands before re-entering reality. I was in Kefalonia years ago—before this book was written—and the author has captured it to a tee. I wish I could say the same about the movie adaptation. Colin and I got into quite a debate one night over the casting of Nicholas Cage in the lead. Colin thought he was perfect. I thought he sounded like 'Honeymoon in Vegas before coming to Greece,'" I rambled, instantly wishing that I could whip out my lip gloss and comb my hair. I could only imagine how awful I looked in my sweatpants, turtleneck, and stocking feet.

"May I join you?" he said. "I'm going to grab a cup of coffee and I'd be happy to get you a refill. You look like you could use a short break."

That said it all. I *did* look awful. I had to run to the ladies room for some damage control.

"Sure, I'd love the company, but it's decaf for me. Excuse me for a minute. I need to powder my nose," I replied.

Oh, God. Powder my nose. No one says that anymore. Why was I finding myself more and more frequently using my mother's expressions? I was turning into her for sure.

I slipped my feet into my running shoes and walked in them, unlaced, to the restroom. I was afraid to look in the mirror. I left home in such a hurry to get started on my holiday that I didn't have time to drag out the big guns. Fortunately, my mother's daughter had some sample cosmetics in her purse. Can't overdo it, though . . . have to look natural.

Yikes! My hair was in ringlets. I guess after I showered, I let it air dry. Well, that's the real me. Why was I feeling like such a schoolgirl on her first date? I had a feeling about this guy. And I was starting to have a feeling about that little Cupid Colin. Was he up to something, I wondered?

I walked back over to the table to see Peter reading the jacket cover of *Corelli's Mandolin*. I smiled as I sat down. I didn't know this man at all, but something told me that he was going to relish this book as much as I did.

"So, it's set on this Greek island, and you've been there, huh? Tell me what some of your favorite islands are," he asked.

"Well, Kefalonia is gorgeous, but it's somewhat new because it was rebuilt after a serious earthquake all but leveled the island in the fifties. So, while it has retained its natural beauty, it's not exactly steeped in antiquity, at least in appearance. It's a rather large island and tranquil, because after the quake so many people fled to other countries altogether. I don't know how to describe it. It's just different.

"Then there's the island of Corfu, which really has quite a Roman influence, being so close to Italy. It's one of the Ionian islands, big and very cosmopolitan. Then there's Zakynthos, which is the only Greek island I've ever been to that I wasn't crazy about. But people argue with me on that one, so I guess I'd give it another try.

"There's Mykonos and Santorini, but they're too touristy, at least in the summer. Crete is a paradise, especially for amateur archeologists. You can't believe the sophisticated bathrooms that they had in 600 B.C. I'd die for a tub like that nowadays. Rhodes is lush and green, very atypical for Greece. Poros . . . well, it's an island for dancers. They start dancing anywhere they want to—in the streets, in tavernas, on the docks. But my absolute favorite is Hydra. I've been there three times. Cars, motorbikes, and even bicycles are banned on the island. You either walk everywhere or take a donkey, if you can find an available one. Most of them, however, are in use, delivering produce and other supplies to the town's shops and restaurants. My favorite memory of Hydra was of a local—a man in about his seventies—sitting on his donkey, hauling his wares while talking on his cell phone. God, I love that island." I took a deep breath.

"I think I'd better get you another cup of decaf. Yours must be cold by now," Peter commented, smiling.

"Oh, I'm so sorry," I blushed. "I've been talking non-stop since I sat down. I guess the topic of Greece does that to me. Then, too, you're easy to talk to. I mean, I hardly know you, but you seem like someone I could talk to for hours. I'm really sorry."

"Don't be. I feel like I could listen to you for hours. I'm getting you more coffee—decaf. I'll be right back," he said.

I watched him walk away and I thought to myself that I wouldn't blame him if he sneaked out the back door—if Beverly's even had a back door. He must think that I'm a total flake, babbling on and on like that. I *am* turning into my mother—in her senior years.

"Here's your coffee, nice and hot. So tell me about Louis de Bernieres' *Corelli's Mandolin* and why you and Colin thought that it was such a great love story," he asked.

"Well, it's about a beautiful woman who lives with her widowed father on the island of Kefalonia and she's engaged to be married to a local, young man. But then the Italians invade Greece during World War II and the young woman falls in love with an Italian captain. Her father, of course, is against the romance. She should stick with her own kind, he argues. He's a very wise man, who understands irresistible desire. But he tries to convince his daughter that passion is transitory while real love is so much more. That's my favorite passage," I continued.

"The one you have memorized?" Peter asked.

"Yes. It's on page 281. I even remember the page. Go ahead— look it up."

"I'd rather not," he said.

"Oh, okay," I replied, quietly. This book might not be for everyone, I thought to myself.

"No, I mean I'd rather hear you recite it."

"Oh no, I can't. Really. I feel like a fool as it is for rambling on and on for the past half hour," I said, feeling the heat rise up in my face.

"Please?" he asked, with his eyes so very blue and pleading.

"Oh, I don't know. No, you may think it's corny—out of context and all. The young woman's father is just talking to her about real love, that's all. It's on page 281," I said.

"Please?" he asked again. "Please?"

My heart was pounding so hard I could feel my pulse throbbing. "Well, okay. Ready? Here goes: 'Love is a temporary madness, it erupts like volcanoes and then subsides. And when it subsides, you have to make a decision. You have to work out whether your roots have so entwined together that it is inconceivable that you should ever part. Because that is what love is. Love is not breathlessness, it is not excitement, it is not the promulgation of promises of eternal passion. It is not the desire to mate every second minute of the day, it is not lying awake at night imagining that he is kissing every cranny of your body. No, don't blush, I am telling you some truths. That is just being *in love*, which any fool can do. Love itself is what is left over when being in love has burned away, and this is both an art and a fortunate accident.'"

I looked down. I had never recited this passage to anyone except myself—sometimes late at night when I couldn't sleep, or to calm myself when I was flying, or when I sat on my balcony in the early morning, watching the sun rise. What made me agree to recite it now to a total stranger, I wondered? I kept looking down. I was too embarrassed and afraid to look up. I stared at my hands, which were trembling on the table. And then, I saw a third hand, reach over to mine. I could feel tears welling up in my eyes, and now I wanted to run right out of Beverly's. But I was frozen. I couldn't speak and I couldn't move.

"Would you do me a favor?" he asked softly. "Would you have dinner with me? You pick the time and the place. It could be right now, or it could be in an hour or two. I don't care. Well, I *do* care really. I'd like it to be right now, but it's only three-thirty in the afternoon, so I guess it wouldn't be time for dinner, but I'll gladly wait. I mean, you could go on with your writing, and I'll leave you alone. I could go over to the other side of the store and start reading my book, and then we could meet up again in a few hours. I'd like to keep talking with you, Francine, if you'd like to, I mean. Will you have dinner with me tonight?"

"Oh, I don't know. No, wait . . . I *do* know. Yes, I'd like that a lot. Let me walk home and just freshen up a bit. I'll meet you back here at five. Would that be alright?" I asked.

"That would be wonderful. I could walk with you, but maybe not yet. I'll just wait for you here. I'll start reading my book, and I'll be here when you get back . . . waiting for you," he repeated.

"Okay," I replied in a small voice.

I scooped my belongings into my backpack and threw my jacket over my shoulders. He gave me a wide grin, and I could feel my face flush again. I rushed out the door of Beverly's and walked at a brisk pace. I couldn't wait to get home so I could hurry back again. I needed to change into something a bit more dinner-appropriate, run a comb through my hair and put on a fresh face. There I go again, turning into my mother. Put on a fresh face. Where did she get that expression? I missed her terribly. And my father . . . and brother . . . and Bob. But moving on while missing them was alright. One didn't negate the other.

As I walked into the lobby of my building, I recalled another one of my mother's favorite expressions: "Good things happen when you least expect them." Riding up in the elevator, I could feel her presence, as if she were standing right next to me. I wondered what she would have said about my day's adventures—and my making a dinner date with a total stranger. She was cautious to a fault, a family trait I undoubtedly inherited. But she was a good judge of character, too, having loved and lived with my father for over forty years, and I somehow felt that she would have approved.

As I unlocked the door to my apartment, I thought about the motherless young girl in *Corelli's Mandolin* and her watchful father, trying to shield his daughter from hurt. I remembered my own parents with their children. Careful . . . sheltering . . . protective. Keeping us from feeling pain. Offering us security. Averting us from risk and, too often in the process, adventure. I recalled my father's final words to me, his motto, whenever I left the house to go anywhere: "Don't get hurt." A heavy if loving admonition.

I thought, too, about my parents' relationship with one another. They had that kind of love—the kind that was left over when "being *in love* has burned away." That's what I was looking for. For the first time in years, I knew what I wanted. I also recognized that heartache and sorrow often travel with chance and uncertainty. But so do hope and joy. They're all part of the journey.

Epilogue

jour.ney (jûŕ nē) n., pl.-**neys**: Travel from one place to another

I'VE GONE ON MANY journeys in my fifty-some years and, while some were more exhilarating, stimulating, exciting, and terrifying than others, all were enlightening. Although none of us remembers it, entering the world is, perhaps, the most intimidating trip of all, as life's unimaginable experiences lie ahead of us. Yet, we survived that first outing, and here we are.

Traveling through childhood, adolescence, college, careers, marriage, birth, and parenting are tremendous journeys for all of us—sweet, complex, uncharted—filled with wonder, discovery, and the insecurities that are inherent in identifying ourselves in new terms . . . ones that previously seemed so foreign. Words like daughter, student, classmate, date, girlfriend, roommate, teacher, partner, significant other, spouse, wife, better-half, responsible party, parent, mommy, mother-in-law, legal guardian. Memories of leaving the hospital with the six-pound, two-ounce bundle that I was responsible for making happy and whole still make me tremble. And, along with these new roles, the subsequent passages of letting go. Literally, of the back of the two-wheeler, as I watched my son's bicycle wobble down the street. Of my daughter, when she insisted that she was old enough to walk to second grade all by herself. A decade later—years that raced by—when I dropped them off at the colleges of their choice where they would spend the next four years fending for themselves and, hopefully, be successful putting their values to the test. Relinquishing a relationship that was supposed to last forever. Or the worst letting go of all: frantically searching in a day or two for the best photos to display or the most poignant words to describe the thirty-one years with my life's partner at his funeral.

In the last year and a half, the journey that I took through Internet dating was the most revealing in terms of learning who I was, where I wanted to go and with whom, what traits I was looking for, in what order, when I'd compromise, when I wouldn't, when or if I'd settle, and in the long run, the realization that I'm the only one who can truly define me. At the end of the day, I'm the one who makes me happy or sad . . . the one who'll shape the rest of my existence. Others can help. They can come in or go out of my life, visit, stay for a while or forever . . . or leave. But, ultimately, I'm the one responsible for finding out what I want, going after it or not, and living my remaining years—decades, hopefully—the way I choose.

All of my Internet dates helped me discover this about myself. The funny ones, the downhearted ones, the young ones, the old ones, the ones who dressed like their kids, the angry ones, the ones who had no interest in me at all, the ones who simply were trying to get through the day, and all of the ones in between. I learned an enormous amount from these men from cyberspace, and I am grateful to each and every one of them. Some of my dates wore their hearts on their sleeves and their frailties on their foreheads. They arrived with their hurt, as they were reeling from abandonment, divorce, or death. And I could relate. They were trying to impress and were hoping to be impressed. They came with their neuroses and their fears . . . with their senses of humor, their stoic natures . . . their excess baggage, and their expectations. In other words, they were just like me. . . and nothing at all like me.

Peter and I met in Beverly's Book Shop eleven months ago. For the first ten months, he was my steady date and people called us a couple. Then, he started talking about a future together, and I found myself changing the subject. I recognized our many differences and knew that we weren't a long-term match. An early-to-bed and early-to-rise guy, Peter preferred living in his remote cottage in the country. I'm a city gal whose body's rhythm revs up at night. His idea of the perfect weekend was reading a book with one eye while watching ESPN with the other. Mine was getting together with friends, listening to live music, or simply engaging in conversation. And it also discouraged me to discover that many of our values were at odds. But it was more than that. I finally wanted to focus on where I was going, instead of with whom.

Although I didn't meet Peter online—we being the unsuspecting objects of that surreptitious matchmaker, Colin—he was somebody's Internet date. Actually, *many* women's Internet date. Yes, prior to meeting me, Peter successfully dated quite a few women—not simultaneously, he assured me—whom he met online. There was the child psychologist, the state senator, the corporate nurse, the college guidance counselor, the marketing consultant, the divorced homemaker, the retired government employee, and the travel agent. As a result of his online exploration, he met a number of interesting women, none of whom he considered to be the perfect match. But he and they had some good times together and, in a few cases, formed lasting friendships. Will he try online dating again? "You bet," he affirmed with much determination, as we parted. Will I? Perhaps.

In searching for a soul mate—the ongoing quest that's supposed to be top priority for all of us who are single—online dating may be one of the venues that I'll pursue. I'll also continue to diversify my social portfolio through family, friends, and colleagues . . . ever-so-gently reminding them that I'm available and haven't given up on being out there. More importantly, I'll let these same friends and family members know that I'm unafraid to be out with myself and that, unless an odd number makes *them* uncomfortable, it no longer makes me feel that way. In a world of twosomes, I'll gladly go to dinners, plays or concerts with any of my coupled friends, just as I'll continue to have fun going to movies, parties, or the symphony alone. Looking for that special someone is still on my itinerary, but it's only one of the stops on my life's tour.

Before my relationship with Peter ended, an acquaintance had remarked, "Isn't that wonderful? Now you'll never be lonely or alone again." I was hoping she'd be right, but somehow I knew better. Although I wasn't alone or lonely with Peter in the beginning, I sensed that I'd be one or both again someday. I know how complicated relationships can be. And I know firsthand how fragile life is. Peter coming into mine wasn't an end to my singular status, but merely a pause. For a while, it was an enjoyable one. Then, our dissimilarities became too important to ignore, and I was on my own, once again. Only this time, it was by choice . . . and it was alright. I knew I would survive. Perhaps even thrive.

I was the voyager. Internet dating was the crossing. And with the excursion's many experiences came an invaluable lesson: Just as I am out there, so, too, is life and it's meant to be explored. It truly is a journey. And although traveling companions can add or detract from the trip—often depending upon pure luck—the adventures are ours and are there for the taking. Life is temporal. It's the journeys that are constant. And they await.

Acknowledgments

I N THE IMMORTAL VOICE of The Divine Miss M, "You've got to have friends, to make that day last long." Mine truly lengthen my days and enrich my life.

I'd like to thank those friends who played an important part in this manuscript, patiently reading every word and graciously offering their feedback: Valjean McLenighan, Jackie Cohen, Lynn Kean, Anne Reusché, and Liz and Richard Brzeczek. Whether traveling with me for most of my life's journey or jumping on board for several of the more recent stops, they and so many others take the time to listen to my stories, share my itinerary, and lend an ear, shoulder, handkerchief, or compass. All my friends are treasures to me.

Writing this book was a trip in itself and introduced me to a number of talented individuals. It was my good fortune to meet Leslie Breed, whose professional advice, responsiveness and diplomacy were second to none. If not for Cheryl Weissman's expertise in untangling my computer wires on several occasions, I undoubtedly would still be on hold for tech support. And Attila Vekony, Will Williams, and Lori Sellstrom deserve medals for their abundance of patience, for which I am most grateful.

I thank my surrogate brother, Marshall Ginsburg, for his candor and sage counsel, always peppered with pointed wit. And my sister-in-law, Lynne Knox, for her kindness and encouragement and for being like my second "chicker." They may have tired hearing from me, but they never let on.

In the end, my reflections come full circle. My parents, James and Frances Pappadis, made enormous sacrifices for my brother Tom, my sister Connie, and me. And speaking of sibs, their love and support sustained me through many travels. What priceless memories our family has had.

I am richly blessed to have my children, Laura and Mark, in my life. Their hearts are big, and good, and kind. I cherish my late-night chats with my daughter-in-law, Sonya. And, of course, Lyla and Emmitt are two of the most precious reasons that I look forward to the years ahead.

Finally, I am grateful to my late husband, Bob, for his profound love, his huge capacity to enjoy life, his infectious humor, and for teaching me the difference between what's really important and what's not. Some called him Rob or Robert; others called him Bobby. All called him a good guy.